RUTH GRAHAM

FEAR NOT TOMORROW, GOD IS ALREADY THERE

...

DEVOTIONAL

100 CERTAIN TRUTHS FOR UNCERTAIN TIMES

HOWARD BOOKS
A DIVISION OF SIMON & SCHUSTER, INC.
New York Nashville London Toronto Sydney

Our purpose at Howard Books is to:
· *Increase faith* in the hearts of growing Christians
· *Inspire holiness* in the lives of believers
· *Instill hope* in the hearts of struggling people everywhere
Because He's coming again!

Published by Howard Books, a division of Simon & Schuster, Inc.
1230 Avenue of the Americas, New York, NY 10020
www.howardpublishing.com

Fear Not Tomorrow, God Is Already There Devotional © 2009 Ruth Graham

Published in association with Ambassador Literary Agency,
Nashville, Tennessee

ISBN 978-1-4165-8663-0

1 3 5 7 9 10 8 6 4 2

HOWARD and colophon are registered trademarks of Simon & Schuster, Inc.

Manufactured in the United States of America

For information regarding special discounts for bulk purchases,
please contact: Simon & Schuster Special Sales at 1-866-506-1949 or
business@simonandschuster.com.

The Simon & Schuster Speakers Bureau can bring authors to your
live event. For more information or to book an event, contact the
Simon & Schuster Speakers Bureau at 1-866-248-3049 or visit our website
at www.simonspeakers.com.

Edited by Cindy Lambert
Interior design by Davina Mock-Maniscalco

Unless otherwise noted, all Scripture quotations are taken from the New
American Standard Bible®. Copyright © The Lockman Foundation 1960,
1962, 1963, 1968, 1971, 1972, 1973, 1975, 1977. Used by permission.
(www.Lockman.org). Scripture quotations marked (KJV) are taken from
the King James Version. Scripture quotations from The Message by Eugene
H. Peterson are copyright © 1993, 1994, 1995, 1996, 2000, 2001, 2002. Used
by permission of NavPress Publishing Group. All rights reserved. Scripture
quotations marked (NLT) are taken from the Holy Bible, New Living
Translation, copyright © 1996, 2004. Used by permission of Tyndale House
Publishers Inc., Wheaton, Illinois 60189. All rights reserved.

Italics in Scripture quotations indicate author's emphasis.

An Invitation for You

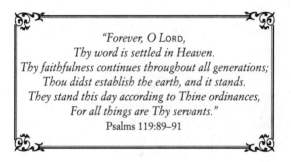

*"Forever, O L*ORD*,*
Thy word is settled in Heaven.
Thy faithfulness continues throughout all generations;
Thou didst establish the earth, and it stands.
They stand this day according to Thine ordinances,
For all things are Thy servants."
Psalms 119:89–91

THOSE ANCIENT WORDS BRING comfort in a world full of uncertainty. We live in uncertain times. It's scary out there. We need only turn on the news, check the balances on our retirement accounts, or look at the brokenness within our own families to be reminded that nothing seems certain. Nothing. But still we long for certainty. We long for something that we can count on. Something to be sure of.

King David, who wrote the above words, lived in an uncertain world. His life was riddled with un-certainty and danger. Family jealousy. Political intrigue. War. Betrayal. Depression. Ridicule. Yet David was secure in the certain knowledge that God was faithful and God's truth eternal. How did he cling to that certain knowledge? Practice. He practiced citing the truth of God's character.

There *are* certain truths we can take hold of and count on. The verse above tells us that God's word is settled—it is a sure thing. Everything else may seem unsettled, precarious, and uncertain, but God's word is sure.

Through His eternal word we can know His character. We can know He is present with us, will lead us, and will hold us securely; that He has a plan for us and it is good. Such truth cannot only chase away the fears that plague us, but can build courage and strength into our lives. To see such certainties, we have to be looking in the right place. We need to turn our eyes toward the Source of Truth: Absolute Truth.

In theory, that sounds so easy. A pat spiritual answer—just focus on God's truth, found in His word, and our fears will just melt away. *So why do I worry and fret? Why is it so hard to trust God during times of uncertainty?* Personal experience has shown me a few uncomfortable realities about myself. I have a short memory for truth when the trials of life pile in on me. I suspect you are the same way. So what, then, is the answer? What will help us remember and apply truth to life when we need it? What will help us conquer our fears?

Practice.

We need to practice God's certain truths over and over again as we meet each new uncomfortable challenge in our lives. Like King David did. Growing in faith is a process—an ongoing lifelong process. It is a choice. A decision we make to take God's truths and apply them to our own life. When fear, worry, and anxiety invade your thoughts and feelings, rather than beating yourself up, recognize that such moments are simply the evidence that God is about to build new faith and strength into your life if only you turn to Him for the wisdom He promises to give to all who ask for it. This is the purpose of this book—to help us consider, focus upon, and practice the certain truths of God.

As I write this, I have just completed the book *Fear Not Tomorrow, God Is Already There*, in which I explore how to trust God in uncertain times. This devotional, which can be used as a companion or follow-up to that book or as a stand-alone book, has provided me with a way to practice and apply God's certain truths in my own life uncertainties. My hope and prayer is that it does the same for you.

I invite you to focus on God's certain truths in your uncertain times.

Ruth Graham

part one

Trust at Your Doorstep

Day 1

Welcome God by Name

> *Those who know Thy name*
> *will put their trust in Thee;*
> *for Thou, O LORD, hast not forsaken*
> *those who seek Thee.*
> Psalm 9:10

WHAT'S IN A NAME? Plenty! We greet one another by name. We introduce people by name. We offer our own names to others when we want to strike up a connection or initiate a conversation. Let's face it. Names matter.

When we read through the Scriptures, we run across whole lists of names. I often wondered why—it makes for rough reading. But God is meticulous about His records and keeping track of names. Names are important to Him. Your name is important to Him.

In Bible times names were significant. They had meaning and were given for a purpose such as a declaration of the parents' desire for a child or as an expression of the parents' convictions or as recognition of divine assistance.

God's names, and there are many, reveal His character. In His Word, God introduces Himself to us through many names: *Mighty Creator, Everlasting God, Prince of Peace, Good Shepherd, Refuge,* and the list goes on. As we come to know His names, we find it easier to put our trust in Him. How can we not trust the One who is the mighty creator, the one who wants the very best for those He made? And what great confidence we can have in One who is everlasting, for though this world and everything in it is temporary, He will never fade away. When we know His names, His character, we want more of Him. We seek Him out. We discover Him.

Did you know that we are told He will not forsake those who seek Him and that while we are seeking, He does not hide? He says, "I love those who love me, and those who diligently seek me will find me" (Proverbs 8.17) He invites us to actively seek Him out. As we do, we will find that we, too, are being sought by the very One we need the most. He will not forsake us—ever.

Take a moment to focus on one of God's names, *The God Who Sees Me.* I love that name! Imagine throwing open the door of your heart and locking eyes with the God who made you and loves you! His loving gaze looks deeply into who you are and loves you unconditionally. How does that truth speak into your situation today? Anticipate your growing trust in God as you discover His true identity.

Heavenly Father,
Thank You that Your names enable me to know
Your character and how You relate to me. I confess
that I don't seek You as I should, but on this day,
Lord, I seek You out and long to know You more
fully. I am grateful that You know my name and
seek me out. You will never forsake me. Thank
You. Amen.

Welcome His Perfect Love

> *There is no fear in love;*
> *but perfect love casts out fear.*
> 1 John 4:18

FEAR. I AM SURE you know it. Probably all too well. We all do. And along with it we know the feelings of anxiety, dread, and worry that accompany fear. As we entertain fear, it grows. It feeds on itself and can swell to control our lives and paralyze us.

Now, in contrast, consider *perfect love*. Can you even imagine such a thing? A love that ensures only the very best for you. What would that kind of love look like to you? A love that makes you feel completely secure and accepted. A love that is comfortable and relaxed, that sets you at ease and fills you with deep joy. Such love is the complete opposite of fear, isn't it? And this scripture tells us that "perfect love casts out fear." This verse seems to imply that they cannot coexist.

Love on earth is imperfect. We know that well. Only God's love is perfect. His love has the power to cast out fear. As we entertain thoughts of His character, His unconditional love, His good plans for us, His grace toward us, and His mercy, fear has to leave, for there is no room for it to stand in the face of such all-encompassing, perfect love.

You can be secure and comfortable in His perfect love. He wants you to be content in His love. He assures you, "I have loved you with an everlasting love; therefore I have drawn you with lovingkindness" (Jeremiah 31:3).

Take a moment to think about what has you afraid today. Then picture the immensity of God's love for you in contrast to that fear. See His gentle love for you. Breathe deeply, and as you exhale, let the fear go—let it slide off your shoulders. Relax and enjoy God's perfect love for you.

Dear loving heavenly Father,
Thank You for Your unconditional, perfect love for
me. I confess that I tend to fear so many things.
You do not want me to live in fear. I am sorry that
I do. Your love has no end, and You have drawn

me to Yourself. I want to concentrate on those certain facts—not on my fear. Please help me to realize and recognize Your perfect love for me. Thank You. Amen.

Day 3

Welcome His Inseparable Love

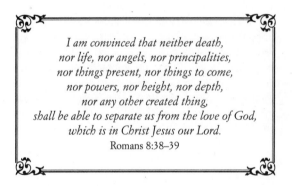

*I am convinced that neither death,
nor life, nor angels, nor principalities,
nor things present, nor things to come,
nor powers, nor height, nor depth,
nor any other created thing,
shall be able to separate us from the love of God,
which is in Christ Jesus our Lord.*
Romans 8:38–39

THE APOSTLE PAUL IS making quite a statement here in these two verses! Does he really mean nothing can separate us from God's love? Yes. Nothing!

You may ask, "What about my sin?" Even that does not separate us from God's love. The Bible tells us that He loved us so much that He sent Jesus, who died for us when we were in sin. Our sin can hinder our relationship with Him. It may hinder our spiritual growth. But for those who believe in Jesus, the Son of God, even our sin does not separate us from His love. He closed that separation through the death and resurrection of His Son. That's amazing! He loves us even in our messed-up lives. Our failures. Our addictions. Our anger. He loves us, and He hurts with us over those things in our lives that keep us from being all He created us to be.   •

Take a moment and think about His love—how all encompassing it is. Think about the fact that His love will never end, never be disappointing, never reject or betray you. What are you facing today? What threat or challenge? Is it big enough to separate you from God's love? No, it is not. He loves you boundlessly! He isn't stingy with His love. He pours it out on you. Hear Him tell you He loves you dearly. Hear His declaration that nothing, absolutely nothing, can separate you from His constant love. Be amazed by His love. Enjoy it.

Heavenly Father,
Thank You for loving me so completely. Not even my sin separates me from Your love. It is hard for me to understand that kind of love. I want to respond to it and be all that You created me to be. I want to confess to You those things that hinder my

relationship with You. I ask You to forgive me and help me move forward into a stronger love relationship with You. Lord, help me pray along with the verse in Romans that "I am convinced." And where I am lacking in faith, Lord, I ask that You convince me. Thank You. And, God, I love You too. Amen.

Day 4

Welcome His Power

> *God hath not given us the spirit of fear;*
> *but of power, and of love, and of a sound mind.*
> 2 Timothy 1:7 (KJV)

FOR THOSE OF US who know the bitter taste of fear and have felt it's icy grip around our hearts, we know how that fear obliterates any sense of power, of security in being loved, and of confidence in right thinking. Fear seeks to snatch away from us the ability to recognize and remember the good things God has given to us. Fear eats away at the very fiber of our being. The enemy of our souls does not want us to know our power over him or the security we have with the God who loves with an everlasting love or the confidence of clear thinking anchored in certain truth. But we do have God's power, God's security, and God's wisdom. It is ours. Available to us for the asking.

But it isn't easy to maintain our certainty, is it? Our enemy is persistent. He looks for any opening to plant fear in our hearts and minds. Today's good news is that we need not fear him "because greater is He who is in you than he who is in the world" (1 John 4:4). It is God in us who gives us victory over fear as we focus on His gentle power, tender love, and compassionate wisdom. Those are antidotes of fear.

Take a moment and recognize what anxiety came to mind. Is there a fear that has you in its icy grip? Maybe it's not something big but something small yet very persistent. A worry that keeps cropping up. An anxiety you cannot seem to shake. It renders you less effective. Makes you feel unsettled. Tends to warp your perspective. Now think about how God sees the thing that tends to consume you. Take a deep breath, and as you let it out, let out all the fear, worry, and anxiety. Then as you inhale, take in the things He has given to you: power, love, and a sound mind. Be still for a moment and let those certain truths settle into your heart. Breathe in His truth today.

Heavenly Father,
Thank You for the gifts You have provided for me.
I confess that I lose sight of them when I am in the
grip of fear. Help me to use Your strong power that

You have placed within me to overcome that fear.
And replace it with Your truth. I want to have
Your perspective so that I can think rightly about
the situations in my life that tie me in knots.
Thank You for giving these wonderful truths to
me. Amen.

Day 5
___

Welcome His Direction

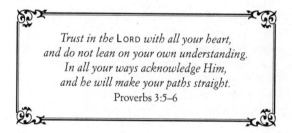

> *Trust in the* Lord *with all your heart,*
> *and do not lean on your own understanding.*
> *In all your ways acknowledge Him,*
> *and he will make your paths straight.*
> Proverbs 3:5–6

Trust is not my default position. When a situation arises, I am quick to fret over finding solutions. I am a fixer, so I leap to trying to figure things out, forgetting that God is already at work in the situation. I jump to conclusions. I strategize, plan, work, and talk, and when things don't move fast enough for me, I try to help them along under my own power. I want to see action, and the truth is, I wear myself out in all my futile attempts to change what I cannot change. That is *leaning on my own understanding.*

That is not God's way. God asks that we trust Him. That's not always easy when decisions need to be made. Which way to go? What to do? Certainly, there are times when we need to take action using our God-given problem-solving skills, but if trust is our foundation, we won't wring our hands, anxiously fearing that we, and we alone, bear the weight of saving every situation from impending disaster. Trust means recognizing that God is actively at work already and that He will shine the light we need to take the next right step. There was a bus company some years ago that had the slogan "Leave the driving to us." We can almost hear God saying it to us: "Leave the control of your life to Me."

Trust Him. He has it figured out. His understanding is infinite. He sees your past, present, and future. He knows you better than you know yourself. And He loves you totally. He will guide you step by step.

Take a moment to remember a time when you were frustrated about a decision. You made one that made sense to you, but you didn't trust God in the process. How did it work out? Did it bring the fulfillment you expected? Did the experience deepen your walk with God, or did you just do it and move on, gaining little? Now think about what you are facing today. Choose to trust God in this moment about this situation. This isn't about answers or quick fixes; this is about choosing to put your finite understanding into His knowing hands and trusting God that He will show you the way.

Heavenly Father,
All too often I wear myself out trying to figure
things out. I live in exhausted frustration. I want
to do what is right, but waiting on You is so diffi-
cult for me. Right now I choose to stop where I am
and trust You. I may not see the answer right now,
but I know You will show me what to do when the
time is right. I am going to quit struggling and
trust You. Thank You ahead of time. Amen.

Welcome His Sufficiency

When I am afraid, I will put my trust in Thee.
Psalm 56:3

I AM GLAD THAT THE psalmist is honest and lets us know there are times when he was afraid. That is one reason I find the Psalms so comforting—he experienced life as I do with all its ups and downs, fears, doubts, joys, and heartaches. He is realistic and lets us know that trusting God does not prevent fear from cropping up in our lives. Fear is part of life. It is a survival instinct. It is a normal response to things we don't understand. But for the psalmist, it seemed to boil down to choices. In spite of the fear, the questions, the doubts, the uncertainty, the pain—in spite of it all—he chose to trust. In the face of fear, he chose to trust. That is not an easy thing to do. But he let us know, set the example, that when he was shaking in his boots, he made a choice. The scripture says, "*I will . . . trust in Thee.*" Life is made up of choices. And the psalmist made his.

We shouldn't think for a moment that all his troubles vanished. They didn't! But what we see is how he changed his focus away from the circumstance that had caused the fear and focused instead on God and His character. I don't know the particular fear that was trying to engulf the psalmist when he wrote those words, but I know that God meets our particular issues with His particular character qualities. Anxiety—calm. Fear—peace. Weariness—rest. Uncertainty—wisdom. Weakness—strength.

Take a moment now and make your own contrasting list. Be particular with what you are facing. Perhaps you are unsure about a decision to be made. He is wisdom. You lack understanding. He is all knowledge. You feel alone. He is near. You are finite. He is infinite. Life is harsh. He is tender.

Make your own list and reflect on it. Make your choice. Then thank Him for the ways His sufficiency fills up your insufficiency.

Heavenly Father,
I am glad that the psalmist was honest about the
fear he experienced. I am afraid too. Life for me is
uncertain, and I am full of anxiety. But right now,
for this moment, I choose to take my focus off of

my problem and turn it to your great character. You are bigger than my problem. You are sufficient when I am not. I trust You to take me where You want me to be, so that I will be the person You created me to be. Help me, Lord, to keep my focus on You. Thank You. Amen.

Welcome His Peace

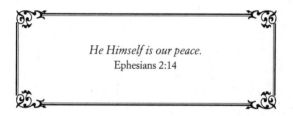

He Himself is our peace.
Ephesians 2:14

W HAT DOES THAT STATEMENT mean? How do we
live in peace when the pressures of living seem
overwhelming? Does it sound to you like a simplistic
platitude? It is not! It is, in fact, a certain truth that
has the power to change our lives.

First, it means that we can relax in knowing that
peace does not come from within us—it is not
something that we have to make happen. It is a gift
from God Himself.

In this chapter of Ephesians, the apostle Paul is
writing about the fact that Jesus died for us while we
were still sinners, still a mess. We were separated
from God; and not only from God but from each
other. Paul uses words like *separate, excluded, no*

hope, and *without God*. Not a pretty picture. Paul actually says we were "dead" in our sins. A barrier divides, leaving some included and some left out. A barrier in a relationship brings hurt and woundedness. Conflict arises, along with separation, exclusion, and hopelessness. How many of us live in such a place, feeling cut off and without much hope?

God does not want us to live that way. In fact, because of God's great mercy and love, He provided Jesus, and His dying for our sin, as the way for the barriers of sin to be broken down and for us to be made alive in God's love.

He is the source of true, lasting peace. True peace does not come from the absence of conflict or stress but from the knowledge in the face of conflict and stress that we have adequate resources. And in Christ Jesus we have all the resources we need: peace, joy, strength, wisdom, love, patience, compassion, grace, and a whole lot more. They are ours—yours for the asking.

Take a moment and ask yourself these questions: Am I at peace with God? Have I been fighting Him? Pushing Him away? Have I let life keep me away from a relationship with Him? Be honest with yourself and with God. If you want God to come into your life with His peace, pray the following prayer:

God of peace,
My life has been in turmoil. I have left You out,
pushed You away, wanting to control my own des-
tiny. But it isn't working out. I am sorry. Please
forgive me and take over my life, including those
parts I keep taking back. I want a relationship of
peace with You. I need Your resources to help me in
the challenges of life. I want your peace in my
heart and mind. Thank You for answering this
prayer. Amen.

Welcome His Help

> *God is our refuge and strength,*
> *a very present help in trouble.*
> Psalm 46:1

THE VERSE ABOVE IS one of the very first verses my mother taught me when I was a child, so it holds a special place in my heart and mind. I am glad she made me memorize it early in my life because I have recalled it many times when I have been afraid or troubled. I love the fact that not only is God a refuge to whom we can go anytime—like running into a safe place—but He is our strength. I don't have to be strong; I have Him. But in addition to knowing that God is our refuge and strength, I love knowing that He is very present in our troubles.

He does not get distracted. He isn't preoccupied. He is very present to our need. He knows what our need is. He wants us to talk to Him about it. He wants us to run to Him when we are afraid and anxious so that He can be our refuge. He wants us to come in our weakness to get His strength. He is our help.

How foolish we are to keep trying to do things our way under the illusion we are on our own, acting in our strength (or trembling in our lack of it) when we have the great God of the universe, our Redeemer, as our refuge, strength, and help. He loves us and is always present with us, paying attention, listening for us.

Take a moment and picture God waiting for you with arms open wide. You are troubled, anxious, running around in circles, and your fear is getting worse with each passing minute. But then you remember this verse—this promise—and you realize you have a safe haven, a place of security where you can get the strength you need to face the day. So you turn and look at Him. Strong. Secure. Loving. As you turn, He opens His arms wide for you to run into them, and as you do, He enfolds you to Himself. You feel the anxiety melt away. The trouble doesn't seem quite so big, because your loving heavenly Father provides you with a place of refuge and gives you His strength. He is very present to your need, very attentive to your situation, and He wants to give you what He is.

Ever-present Father,
Thank you that you are my refuge—a place of
security. You will never let me down. And You are
my strength. I confess that I have been trying to do
things on my own. I am tired. Forgive me for not
coming to You sooner. I come in my weakness and
fear, asking You to fill me with Your strength—
with Yourself. Thank You for being a very present
help for me. Amen.

part two

Discover His
Trustworthiness

Trust His Nearness

Those who follow after wickedness draw near;
they are far from Thy law.
Thou art near, O LORD,
and all Thy commandments are truth.
Psalm 119:150–151

BESIDE THOSE VERSES IN the margin of my Bible I have written "anxiety, fear." In other words, anxieties and fears are wicked, and they pursue me relentlessly. Satan uses them effectively to keep me in turmoil and derail my effectiveness for God. He tries to keep me away from God's truth that He is near. It is a battle. But we are assured that He is near.

For more confirmation, check out this certain truth in Psalm 145:18–19: "The LORD is near to all who call upon Him, to all who call upon Him in truth. He will fulfill the desire of those who fear Him;

He will also hear their cry and will save them." That is truth. His nearness is part of His character—it is an attribute of God. He is near. That is a comfort you can count on. He does not abandon or forsake us. He will not fail. He will not disappoint. He does not reject or betray. He is worthy of our trust.

Psalm 9:10 tells us, "Those who know Thy name will put their trust in Thee; for Thou, O LORD, hast not forsaken those who seek Thee." Knowing God's name seems to be a prerequisite for putting our trust in God. His name reveals His character, and as we know His character, we discover that He is worthy of our trust.

The psalmist tells us that He will not forsake those who seek Him. *Seeking* is an active word. We must seek God. And while we are seeking, He does not hide. He tells us that He came "to seek and to save that which was lost." I picture in my mind a person lost in the woods, frantically seeking a place of safety, only to round the bend and find that she was being sought by the very One she needed the most.

Take a moment and still your heart and mind. Are you seeking God? Hear God tell you that He is near to you. Even in the midst of difficulties.

Heavenly Father,
Thank You that You are near. Thank You that Your
name reveals Your great, unchanging character
and that Your Word is truth that I can use effec-
tively to renew my mind. When I call out to You,
Lord, I do not have to be caught in a cycle of anxi-
ety and fear, for You hear me, and I know You are
near. I can know You and Your ways. I want to
know You and Your nearness even more. Amen.

Trust His Ability

> *Now to Him who is able to do exceeding abundantly*
> *beyond all that we ask or think . . .*
> Ephesians 3:20

WHO WANTS TO RELY on someone who isn't able to do what was promised? Empty promises are all too common. Broken promises wound. Unmet expectations make us cynical. No. We don't want to rely on someone who cannot fulfill his word. That's why I love all the promises in Scripture that tell me God is able. And this verse in Ephesians could not be more expansive. He is able to do exceeding abundantly above all that we ask or think. It would be enough for Him to do "exceeding abundantly." But He adds that He does much more than that. He does more than our imaginations can fathom—more than we can even ask. Wow!

Now, we are not talking wishes here. We are speaking of realities in the spiritual realm. And He is more, so much more, than we can imagine. His love is greater. His grace is wider. His mercy is deeper. Everything about Him is beyond our ability to imagine. He is a great and awesome God who chooses to be able, not only in His creation of the world and His power to rule it, but in our lives, our circumstances, our challenges.

Take a moment and think about where you need God to be able for you right now. Are you weary of the struggle of life and need joy? He is able. Are you alone and need someone's presence? He is able. Are you half sick with worry for a loved one and need assurance? He is able. Are you facing a major decision and don't know which way to turn? He is able. Open your Bible and ask God to take you to promises that speak to your need. Then claim them as your own. Write your name in them. Pray them back to God. My mother used to tell me, "All the promises of God are on the believer's side." He wants you to know firsthand that "He . . . is able to do exceeding abundantly beyond all that we ask or think."

Able Father,
I have experienced disappointment. I face chal-
lenges that seem daunting, are above what I am
able to accomplish under my own power. You say

*that You are able to meet my need. Today I am
facing _____. Please help me. I want to trust You.
I want to know firsthand that You are able. I want
to take a step out onto the ice. But I am afraid.
Please help me to trust You and grow in that trust.
Thank You. Amen.*

Trust Him with the Impossible

> *Nothing will be impossible with God.*
> Luke 1:37

ARE YOU FACING SOMETHING today that looks impossible? Bills that have mounted beyond your ability to cope? A life-threatening illness? A loved one on a destructive downward spiral? Are you overwhelmed with a too busy schedule and daily demands? It all looks impossible. It probably is.

God is famous for allowing people to find themselves in impossible situations. Daniel in the lions' den. Joseph facing the pregnancy of Mary. A child promised to a childless Abraham and Sarah. Shadrach, Meshach, and Abednego in the fiery furnace. Paul shipwrecked. I wouldn't choose to be in any of those situations. But it is amazing to see what God did through them—He revealed His glory and

His ability. He does great things in impossible situations!

Daniel, Joseph, Abraham, the three men in the fiery furnace, and Paul all had something in common—they trusted God. In the face of the impossible, they believed God. They knew that the odds were against them; they knew the situation was impossible but they also knew the kind of God they served. They knew His character, so they focused on it rather than on the impossibility of their circumstances. He does great work with the impossible. Jesus Himself was born into an impossible situation.

As I consider the many seemingly impossible situations recounted in the Bible where God accomplished His purposes by doing the impossible, I discover one common element. Over and over again, God's mighty acts, His solutions, differed greatly from what the men and women in those situations expected or believed was needed. The same has been true in my own life. As we grow in our trust of God, we discover that He is not a magician at our disposal to perform impossible feats of our choosing. Rather He is the all-knowing God who surprises us with His solutions to the impossible events in our lives. The key, then, is to look expectantly toward God in the midst of our impossibilities and trust Him that He is at work for our eternal good.

Take a moment and think about the impossibility you are facing. Then think about the verse above—"nothing will be impossible with God." Nothing. He can take what you are facing and reveal to you His power, His will, and His work in that situation. As God's work in your impossible challenge unfolds, keep a record of how He worked. This will help build your faith as you remember His work in the midst of your next impossible situation.

God of the impossible,
You know the impossibility I am facing. I just
cannot see my way through it. The scripture says
nothing is impossible with You. I release the situation to You to work in it as You see fit. I am going
to trust Your character and wait for You to work it
out for Your glory. Help me to be patient and grow
in trust. Thank You. Amen.

Trust That He Is Changeless

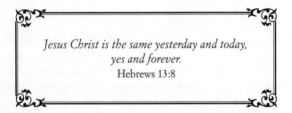

Jesus Christ is the same yesterday and today,
yes and forever.
Hebrews 13:8

THE ONE SURE THING is change! I don't like change,
I admit. Yet change is inevitable. Change makes
me feel insecure. The weather changes. My body
changes. My health changes. Government leaders
change. Relationships change. The earth changes.
Even the universe changes, scientists tell us.

Often we fight change or ignore it. Like age, failing eyesight, hearing loss, weight. But in the end, everything changes. The lack of change is just an
illusion we buy into because it gives us a sense of security—false though it be.

It is hard to imagine something that doesn't
change. In the seventies I lived near Philadelphia and

would frequently go into New York City. The Twin Towers were being built. It was interesting to see them grow taller month by month until they dominated the skyline of that great city. We all thought they would be there forever. They were part of our national symbols of freedom and capitalism.

None of us will forget how we felt as we watched in disbelief as those majestic towers came thundering down. I stood in my living room and for the first time as an American felt very insecure. Our lives changed that day, and the world would never be the same.

It is difficult to trust in things that change. Trust is built on the assurance of constancy. Today's verse tells us that Jesus never changes. He is constant. Jesus is the exact representation of God, so we know God's character does not change. His mercy, peace, forgiveness, joy—all are always there and always available.

Take a moment to reflect on the changes you are currently experiencing in your life. Think about the uncertainty they create. Read this verse again, and ask the Holy Spirit to engrave it on your heart and in your mind so that in the face of life's uncertainties, you will know the security of God's changeless nature.

Changeless Creator,
So much is changing all around me. Uncertainty
makes me feel afraid. I find trust difficult, and so I

grasp for control. I want to know Your changeless character more fully so that I will trust You more and more. You say You are the same yesterday, today, and every tomorrow. Please reveal that to me in a concrete way this week. Thank You. Amen.

—

Trust His Provision

---

*My God shall supply all your needs according
to His riches in glory in Christ Jesus.*
Philippians 4:19

I LOVE HOW THE APOSTLE Paul begins this verse
with "My God." It is such a personal, relational
statement. Clearly Paul is not writing about some
aloof deity, but about his God, the God he knows
and trusts. God knows you and is interested in your
personal need. He promises to supply, provide for,
your needs. And not just the bare minimum, but in
abundance.

But let's face it, we are impatient people, aren't
we? We'd like to have it all, ahead of schedule and according to our specifications so we can relax and not
fret or be anxious. We want the supply fulfilled according to our point of view, not necessarily God's

point of view. If I asked my mother for ten cookies, she might have given me an apple—not what I asked for but what I needed for my own health and well-being.

"According to His riches in glory" implies an endless supply. Vast. Beyond comprehension. If we cannot comprehend the universe, then we cannot comprehend the vastness of His supply. It is there for us—at our disposal—as we trust Him.

Jesus Christ is the channel for those supplies— He is the key component. On one side we have our needs—be they financial, physical, or emotional— and on the other side is God's vast supply. The bridge is Jesus Christ. He is the conduit. We put our trust in His ability and willingness to provide for us. We do it by faith, knowing He will do what is best for us and show us His way.

Take a moment and think of the needs in your past and how God has supplied from the store-house of His riches. Remember a time when He met your need in a way that may have been differ-ent than you expected but was far better than you dreamed. Choose to trust Him now in the circum-stance in which you find yourself. Almighty God provided in the past and will in the present and fu-ture.

God of great provision,
I am overwhelmed by my own needs and the needs
of those around me. I know I do not have the
needed resources, but You do. You are willing to
meet my needs through Jesus in ways that are best
for me. Thank You for doing it in the past. I trust
You for today and tomorrow. Thank You. Amen.

Trust His Communication

> *The Lord used to speak to Moses face to face,*
> *just as a man speaks to his friend.*
> Exodus 33:11

GOD LOVES TO COMMUNICATE with us. Back in the Garden of Eden, He talked with Adam and Eve. He enjoyed this fellowship with them. Then that fellowship was broken by sin. Yet God, longing for fellowship with humanity, devised a plan whereby that intimacy could be restored. God is a God of communication. God is a God of relationship. There is no greater example of that than when God sent Jesus to Earth to communicate His love for us. God broke into history and spoke His Word to His people.

He came near to us, became one of us. God came down to our level to talk with us. To tell us and show us the depth of His love and grace. Not only did God come to us, but He came in a form to which everyone could relate. He came as a baby.

Almighty God, Creator, Maker, wants to speak to you "just as a man speaks to his friend." How do you speak to your dearest friends? Do you call your friend, read off a list of worries and wants, and hang up? Of course not! You dialogue. Friends communicate with each other, both speaking, both listening, responding to each other, asking each other questions, and even noticing the unspoken messages.

How is your dialogue with God doing lately? Have you considered actual dialogue with God, where He speaks and you listen, then you speak and He listens? Are you spending time actually listening? So often we are so busy talking that God can't get a word in edgewise! You have to be quiet, still your heart, and listen. Read His Word, and listen. Do His will, and listen. He will speak to you—through the Scriptures, through a person, through an experience, by an impression in your mind. God speaks in the way that you can best hear Him.

Take a moment and remember a time when you knew God was speaking to you. What was going on? Where were you? How did He speak to you? What did He tell you? Write the answers to these questions in your journal, and then take note each time you hear from God. This record will be an encouragement for you. as you discover how many ways God communicates to you. He wants to talk with you personally. And He wants you to talk to Him—as you would to a friend. That's how you will get to know Him.

Intimate Father,
Thank You for being a God who communicates
personally and individually with me. I want to
know You better and develop a closer friendship
with You. I confess that I am not very good at qui-
eting myself in order to hear You. Help me to do
that. Give me attentive ears to hear and a willing
heart to act on what You say to me. Thank You.
Amen.

Day 15

Trust His Instruction

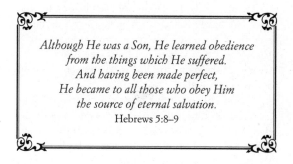

Although He was a Son, He learned obedience
from the things which He suffered.
And having been made perfect,
He became to all those who obey Him
the source of eternal salvation.
Hebrews 5:8–9

I DON'T LIKE THE WORD *obey*. It insults my independence. I want to be in control. In fact, I tend to be willful, and I recognize a disobedient streak in my heart. How about you?

There is a local television station that regularly has children speaking into the camera. It can be fun to hear how children perceive the world. But the station's motto, "W— puts children first" brings to mind that all too often our society is wrongly putting children's material desires and momentary

happiness above their well-being and training. Our
society is infected with an "I come first" and "I am a
god" mentality, and it starts with the assumption
that we "should" get what we want, when we want
it. Willfulness, self-centeredness, and seeing ourselves as greater than we are are perhaps among the
most glorified and misunderstood sins we face
today.

We are not gods. We do not even belong to ourselves. We have been created by God who designed
us with a purpose. We have been bought for a
price—the precious blood of Jesus (see 1 Peter 1:19).
We are not independent. We are dependent on God
for our very breath.

Just as children must learn obedience—to sub-
ject their willfulness to someone greater than themselves—for their own good, so, too, we must learn to
obey God's instruction for our own best interest.
Obedience is yielding our wills to another even when
we don't understand why. He always knows what is
best for us and doesn't hesitate to require obedience.
He is not out to make us happy, but to make us holy.

Jesus is our example. He practiced obedience to
the point of death on a cross. He wrestled with obedience in the garden of Gethsemane. He did not
want to suffer and die, but He yielded to the will of
His Father. In doing so, He opened the way for our
salvation.

Take a moment and consider what you are holding back from God today. What is God asking you to
do? Why are you resisting? Be very honest with your-

self and with God. Seek godly counsel, then choose to obey no matter the consequences.

Loving heavenly Instructor,
Thank You that Jesus yielded His will to Yours—
that He was obedient. I confess that I am stubborn
and willful. I like things my own way. Forgive me
for whining when I don't get my way. I choose to
obey You even when I don't understand, because I
know You know what is best for me. Thank You.
Amen.

Trust His Patience

*The Lord is not slow about His promise,
as some count slowness,
but is patient toward you,
not wishing for any to perish
but for all to come to repentance.*
2 Peter 3:9

PATIENCE MEANS TO ENDURE the unpleasantness of a delay in what you want, without complaint or anger; to remain calm and willing to wait when you do not yet have that for which you are hoping. I usually look patient and calm, but the truth is, that is just a facade. Inside I am full of anxiety. I must confess that I am impatient. When I see something that needs doing, I get to it, and if someone doesn't do something in the time I think it needs to be done, I get agitated. Not a good thing!

God is very patient. Throughout Scripture we see His patience. Look at how patient He was with the nation of Israel. He gave them His visible presence in the pillar of fire by night and the cloud by day. But that wasn't enough for them. He gave them Moses as their leader, but they grumbled against his leadership. He provided food and water in the desert, but they complained that there wasn't any variety. The Bible says their shoes didn't even wear out! He continued to perform miracle after miracle to show them His love and goodness. And almost at every chance they got, they complained and grumbled. They were dissatisfied with the way He did things and the time it took, so they made the golden calf. They got homesick for Egypt and slavery. They did everything wrong.

Did God give up on them? No. Did He punish them? Yes. But He never gave up on them. He was faithful and patient because He had the larger view in mind, which was to have a chosen people from which His Son would be born, live, and die to redeem all mankind. He saw beyond the Hebrew tribes as slaves in Egypt, beyond all the prophecies, to the fulfillment in Christ the Messiah. And even now, we may think He is slow, but He sees beyond today to the fulfillment of all of history when Jesus will return to set up His kingdom on Earth. His will is being patiently fulfilled. He carries out His purposes in His time and in His way—and His way is always perfect.

Take a moment to look back and see how God

has worked in your life in the last year: the money that came just in time, the phone call that made a difference, the contact that opened a door, the accident that was avoided . . . Did you stop to thank Him? Do so now.

Patient Father,
Thank You for never tiring of my inadequacy and
needs for constant reassurance. I confess that I
often take situations into my own hands without
waiting for You and Your will for my life. Forgive
me for my impatience, and teach me to be more
steadfast. Thank You. Amen.

part three

Experience His Presence

His Presence Sets You Free

> *There is therefore now no condemnation*
> *for those who are in Christ Jesus.*
> Romans 8:1

HAVE YOU EVER WALKED into a group where you immediately felt disapproved of—you just didn't belong? Or maybe there is a person whom you know disapproves of you. I am quite sure you don't like to spend time with that person. It's very uncomfortable to be in his or her presence. Maybe you feel that way about God. Deep down in your heart of hearts you feel He disapproves of you because of a cycle of sin you cannot seem to escape.

The apostle Paul had just been writing about how wretched he felt because of his sin. He said, "Wretched man that I am! Who will set me free from the body of this death?" (Romans 7:24). We've been there! We have a monkey of repetitive sin on our backs and can't seem to get loose. We feel that we keep doing the same sin, the same wrong, again and again. We feel like there is no way out! Paul felt that way. It made him feel wretched.

But then he declares, "Thanks be to God through Jesus Christ our Lord!" (Romans 7:25). In chapter eight he declares that for those of us who have made Jesus our Lord, we are not under condemnation. We are free! He says there is *no* condemnation—not even a little bit. We can live free. As a matter of fact, Paul goes on to say, "For the law of the Spirit of life in Christ Jesus has set you free from the law of sin and of death" (8:2). That is good news—wonderful news!

That feeling of condemnation is from the Enemy! That negative self-talk is from Satan! There is a difference between conviction of the Holy Spirit and condemnation from Satan. We must pay attention to conviction and take it to the Lord in repentance. But then there is no condemnation. We can move forward in freedom and not look back. When the Son sets us free, we are truly free. Enjoy the freedom.

Take a moment and write down the things about which you feel condemned. Ask God to help you discern what is condemnation from the Enemy and what is conviction from Him. If it is conviction, repent and ask for forgiveness. If it is condemnation, then let it go. Quote the above scripture to Satan. Tell the Enemy that you will not tolerate his influence in your life—you have been set free! And thank God for it.

Heavenly Father,
I struggle with self-disapproval and feel so bur-
dened by condemnation. I condemn myself for not
being "good enough" and grow frustrated with my
efforts. This is not my burden to carry, and I thank
You for setting me free in Jesus Christ. Amen.

His Presence Never Deserts You

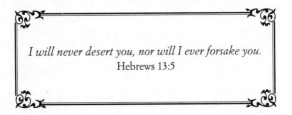

I will never desert you, nor will I ever forsake you.
Hebrews 13:5

WE ALL FEAR ABANDONMENT. If we are honest, we all have fears of being deserted, cut off, and left alone. Those fears are part of our sinful self. Perhaps you know the feeling of depending on people only to find they weren't there for you. You felt betrayed. Perhaps you have known rejection by a loved one. Or perhaps you are afraid that if people knew what you were really like, they would drop you like a hot potato. We try to cover up the real us, and we put on our masks for fear that if we are truly known, we will experience rejection.

That is not the case with God. He knows you better than you know yourself. He can read your thoughts. The psalmist says, God is "intimately acquainted with all my ways." There is nothing we can hide from Him, and the wonderful thing is that He still loves us intensely. He delights in us and promises never to desert us, never abandon us. He will never forsake us. Not only does He not forsake, but He is constantly with us. His presence in our lives is truly permanent for all eternity.

In Matthew 28:20 Jesus says, "I am with you always, even to the end of the age." That is security. That is constancy. His presence is something we can depend on. As I write this, it is New Year's Day. I face a new year with many uncertainties. And as I look at the future, I know that regardless of the uncertainties or troubling circumstances or joys that may come this year, one thing that is certain is, God is going to be with me. His presence will always be constant, not just near me but inside me. The Holy Spirit resides in the heart of every believer, so consequently we can never be separated from God. I may not feel His presence all the time, but I know He is there. It is a fact, because He has said He will never desert me or forsake me, and God does not lie. We can count on God to keep His promises.

Take a moment to thank God for His presence with you right now. Then picture in your mind some situations you are facing—as if you were walking into an unknown room. You may feel fear, intimidation, and anxiety. As you hesitantly open the door, you feel a friend come alongside you to give you courage. That friend walks into the room with you, and you are no longer afraid or anxious, because he is with you. See that friend as God's presence.

Everpresent heavenly Father,
Thank You for Your promise never to leave me or
forsake me. I confess that I often live as if You are
not with me. I actually forget about You. Help me
not to forget, but to be ever mindful of Your pres-
ence with me. Thank You. Amen.

His Presence Is Your Dwelling Place

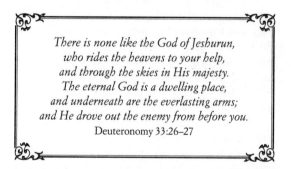

> *There is none like the God of Jeshurun,*
> *who rides the heavens to your help,*
> *and through the skies in His majesty.*
> *The eternal God is a dwelling place,*
> *and underneath are the everlasting arms;*
> *and He drove out the enemy from before you.*
> Deuteronomy 33:26–27

I LOVE THIS PICTURE OF God! Just imagine this awesome Being—none other like Him—who rides throughout the heavens to be your help. He gathers His majestic self to be with you. Can you imagine walking into a great palace of a mighty king and having him run down the corridor with all his authority and majesty to be with you? To invite you to live there with him? Wow! That is what this verse is saying. You are important to God.

What a promise from God! It tells us so much about His character. He is eternal in His authority, power, and majesty. All that He is will never quit or run out. He is awesome and to be revered. It is this same God who invites you to dwell with Him. He is tender and protective of you. And He is the one who fights your battles for you.

Though my earthly address has changed often, I know what my true address is. God. He is my dwelling place. My home. My place of safety and security. He holds me safely in those mighty, eternal arms. He will not let me go. I have had precious moments in my life when my earthly father held me in his arms. I needed his warmth, strength, tenderness, and protection. But he had to let me go. God never does.

How do we dwell with God? The same way we learn to dwell with other people. We invite them in. We learn what they like and don't like. We talk to them. We listen to them. We remove things from our home that cause them to be uncomfortable or are offensive. It is the same with God. We develop a dwelling place with Him by daily cultivating a relationship with Him. We do that by reading and studying His Word, listening for His voice, talking to Him, and obeying Him. As we dwell with Him, He drives out the enemies we face.

Take a moment and ask yourself where you live. Do you live in your own strength, trying to do it all yourself? Do you live in fear and anxiety? God invites you to live in His presence, and He gives to you all that He is. He loves you. He will guide you, protect you, and hold you securely.

Gracious Father, my Dwelling Place,
I confess that I live in my own neighborhood of
fear, distraction, anxiety, fatigue. I am tired of
trying to handle it all myself. I want to dwell with
You. I turn my life over to You. Please drive out the
enemies that seek to keep me in defeat. Thank You
for making a room for me with You. I look forward
to getting to know You better. Amen.

His Presence Gives Rest

---

*My presence shall go with you,
and I will give you rest.*
Exodus 33:14

GOD HAD GIVEN MOSES the task of leading the
Hebrew nation out of Egypt to the land He had
promised them. It was a daunting task to say the least.
There were many obstacles, battles to fight, rebellions
to deal with, insurrections, discontent, ingratitude
(very much like being a parent!). Moses, no doubt,
was fed up with these people and very tired at this
point in the book of Exodus. Discouraged. Moses
wanted reassurance, and he was very honest with
God about his needs.

How often I am at that place. I need reassurance
as a parent when the going gets tough. I am desper-

ate to know God is with me. I need some help, and yet I try to keep up the pretense even with God that I have it under control. Is that where you are? You are scared. Are you ready to quit? Maybe you already have. This isn't what you bargained for. You feel forgotten and alone. Worn out. It all seems overwhelming; you are tired, and you want out!

God understands when we reach the end of our rope. God reassures Moses in this verse with the certain truth that God's very own presence is going to be with him. He is not alone. He doesn't have to battle in his own strength. The psalmist tells us "in Thy presence is fulness of joy" (Psalm 16:11). Living in His presence enables us to experience joy no matter what the circumstances. Not only is He going to go with him, but He is going to give Moses rest. I like the sound of that!

This kind of rest does not mean vacation from responsibilities or cessation of work—as nice as that would be. It is a rest given in the midst of the struggle; the rest that comes when our minds, hearts, imaginations, and principles are working in harmony. It is the satisfaction in knowing we have done our best.

Yes, God not only promises to go with us, but to also give us rest. What a wonderful promise!

Take a moment and quiet yourself. Ask God to help you if it is difficult for you to get quiet. Think about the challenges you face this week. Tell God honestly about your thoughts and feelings. He truly understands and is ready to help you—He goes with you into that difficult situation not only to help you, but to give you rest in the process.

Holy Father of rest,
Thank You for this wonderful promise. I claim it
for myself. I confess that I try to do it all on my
own and pretend that I have it under control. I
don't. I am discouraged, angry, and ready to quit.
Please forgive me. Help me to believe You are with
me and will give me the rest I need in the midst of
the situation I now face. Thank You. Amen.

His Presence Is Continuous

> *I have set the* LORD *continually before me;*
> *because He is at my right hand,*
> *I will not be shaken.*
> Psalm 16:8

WHAT DO YOU LOOK at every day? What do you listen to every day? What do you talk about daily? What is continually before you? It is very important what we let press into our hearts and minds each day. The psalmist said that He set the Lord continually before him. Continually. Not just occasionally. Not just sometimes. But constantly, repeatedly, persistently, without ceasing. What does that mean? How do we do that? Is that even a realistic expectation? Can we do that practically? After all, we have lives to live, schedules to keep, people to see.

The psalmist says he does this because the Lord is at his right hand. He places the Lord near to his thoughts and behavior. How can we do that? We set the Lord continually before us by reading and memorizing His Word. I keep verses on my bathroom mirror, by my kitchen sink, and in my car to read, review, and memorize throughout the day. I listen to praise music in my office and home—there is always something near to draw my thoughts to God. I talk with my friends about what He is teaching me, or I discuss something I learned in my quiet time that morning. I pray all day long—just in and out conversations—as I go through my day. It isn't complicated. It involves consistency and keeps Him continually before me. And when we are living in the awareness of His mighty presence, we will not easily be shaken.

I do not do it perfectly. Far from it. There are a million distractions. That is why I place reminders around me. And I know that when I fail because my thinking gets muddled and I become dual minded, God does not. He is right there waiting for me to acknowledge His presence.

Take a moment to acknowledge His presence with you right where you are. Read today's verse again. Write down some practical ways you can set Him continually before you. Then begin to put them into practice.

Guiding Father,
Help me to live continually in Your presence. Help
me to establish habits that place You at my right
hand. Forgive the many times I rush into my day
not acknowledging You, then wonder why I get
shaken. I want to change that, and I ask You to
help me. Thank You. Amen.

His Presence Reassures You

Have not I commanded you?
Be strong and courageous!
Do not tremble or be dismayed,
for the LORD *your God is with you wherever you go.*
Joshua 1:9

JOSHUA IS ABOUT TO step into Moses' shoes and take over the leadership of God's people to take them into the Promised Land. Can you imagine taking Moses' place? God chose Joshua for this position, and Joshua had proven himself as an able leader. God told Joshua to be strong and courageous. But perhaps now there was a weakening and he wasn't feeling so strong and courageous.

He looked out over the mass of people he was to lead. He looked back, and Moses was no longer there. He was no doubt feeling alone, inadequate, and intimidated. He looked down and saw shaky knees. He had stepped up in obedience, but now he needed reassurance.

Joshua had a personal relationship with God. God was no stranger to him. And God, of course, knew exactly what Joshua was feeling. I take comfort in this verse as God reminds Joshua that He had told him to be courageous and strong. He knew Joshua's need for reassurance. "Do not tremble or be dismayed." I do not see harshness here or rebuke. I picture God putting His arms around Joshua and telling him, "I am with you wherever you go." God is kind and gentle. God was not going to abandon him now—far from it. He would be with him every step of the way.

I think I have something in common with Joshua. I need God's reassurance over and over again as I face things that appear overwhelming. How about you? Do you long for God's reassurance today?

Take a moment and write down what has you shaking in your shoes today. Be specific. Now look up these three Scripture selections: Matthew 28:17–20, Psalms 34:7, and John 14;16–20. Read them, inserting your name and your circumstance into your dialogue with God. Listen for God's reassurance that He will not let you down. Today's certain truth is that He is with you wherever you go, and He doesn't abandon you when you need Him most.

Reassuring Father,
I try to be strong and courageous. But I confess
that I weaken in my resolve. I am afraid of what
lies ahead for me. I need Your reassurance. I claim
this promise that You made to Joshua that You will
be with me wherever I go. Thank You. Amen.

Day 23

His Presence Is Holy

> *As obedient children,*
> *do not be conformed to the former lusts*
> *which were yours in your ignorance,*
> *but like the Holy One who called you,*
> *be holy yourselves also in all your behavior.*
> 1 Peter 1:14–15

GOD IS A HOLY god. In heaven the anthem rings out, "Holy, holy, holy, is the Lord God, the Almighty" (Revelation 4:8). Holiness is His nature. It informs all of His other characteristics. It makes Him wholly other than us.

When we think of holiness, we think of perfection. God is perfect. We think of purity. God is totally pure. We think of worship. God is worshipped. Maybe the idea of holiness puts us off. We can't relate to holiness and perfection. God knew that. That is why He sent Jesus to show us what God was really like. Holiness didn't keep Jesus from hanging out with sinners. It didn't make Him unapproachable.

So what does Peter mean when he tells us to be holy in all our behavior? How can he tell us to be holy like God? We can't be perfect or pure—hard as we try, we are still sinners. However, we can nurture holiness by the choices we make. To be holy means to operate by another frame of reference—a heavenly one rather than an earthly one. No longer is the burning question, "What pleases man?" but, "What pleases God?" God calls us to accept the consequences and responsibilities of living a holy life. It means freedom and joy that come from not measuring our success, value, or wealth by earthly standards.

God used sinners to further the kingdom of God. People like Abraham, Jacob, David, Peter, Paul, a prostitute, and a tax collector, to cite a few. He could use them because they knew they were sinners and in need of God's forgiveness and grace. They knew what it was to be broken and find grace rather than condemnation. The world condemned and discounted them. God did not. He chose to redeem them and use them. "God has chosen the foolish things of the world to shame the wise" (1 Corinthians 1:27). God's holiness operates on a different standard. Let us choose to do the same.

Take a moment and think about the ways you operate on earthly values. Ask God to help you reorient your thinking to His ways. Choose one thing to begin to work on today. Read Philippians 4:4–9 to discover what God would have you thinking about. You may want to write verse 8 on an index card and post it in a place where you will see it as an encouragement and reminder to choose His way of holiness.

Holy God,
I want to operate on heavenly standards but I fall back into old habits and old ways of thinking. Forgive me. I ask You to change me so that You can use me to further Your kingdom in my home, neighborhood, office, and school. Thank You.
Amen.

His Presence Is Inescapable

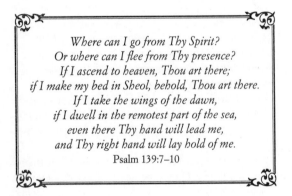

Where can I go from Thy Spirit?
Or where can I flee from Thy presence?
If I ascend to heaven, Thou art there;
if I make my bed in Sheol, behold, Thou art there.
If I take the wings of the dawn,
if I dwell in the remotest part of the sea,
even there Thy hand will lead me,
and Thy right hand will lay hold of me.
Psalm 139:7–10

DAVID IS NOT TRYING to flee God's presence. He asks a philosophical question: Is it possible to get away from God's presence? Heaven? Nope, God is there. Hell? Nope, God was there. Can I go beyond the sunrise? Nope. God is there too. How about going into the deepest part of the oceans? Nope. God is there. His presence is higher, deeper, and wider than anything we can encounter. It is not just in physical places but emotional places as well. In our highs and lows. Our joys and sorrows. Also in our spiritual places. Times when we feel God is absent or silent. Times when we feel on top of the world.

But hell? That seems like a contradiction. You may ask, "Isn't a definition of hell as the absence of God's presence?" David clearly says that if we go into hell, He is there. How many of us have had our own personal emotional hell? Abuse. Betrayal. Financial ruin.

Loss of reputation. Or a physical hell? Chronic pain. Illness. God is there with you. Graciously, God sent His Son to hell so that we won't ever have to experience absence from God's presence. Jesus went there to set the captives free. He obtained the victory over everything—including your own personal hell. You are free.

Perhaps you have tried to run away from God. You cannot flee. He follows after you to draw you to Himself. And He is persistent. He has been called "the hound of heaven." He is not limited by time or space. He knows where you live and seeks you out. Nothing you have done creates a distance too great for God to touch your life with His forgiveness and restoration. Nothing can separate you from His love—absolutely nothing. Yield to His gracious love, and find the freedom for which you truly long.

Take a moment to ask yourself where you would go to get away from God. Have you tried? Now think of God's inescapable presence. Acknowledge that He is with you right now. He is all that you need Him to be right this minute. His love and presence are inescapable. Take joy in knowing that you are secure, totally known, and totally loved.

Inescapable Father,
Thank You that there is nowhere I can go to get
away from You. I need Your presence. I need to
know that You are there like You promised. I want
Your presence to bring comfort, but I confess that
at times it scares me. Even though I don't feel wor-
thy enough to be in your presence, I accept by faith
that You accept me. Amen.

part four

Know His Comfort

The Comfort of His Rejoicing

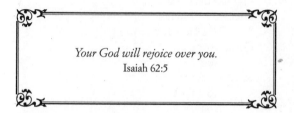

Your God will rejoice over you.
Isaiah 62:5

HEAR THIS FROM GOD, let Him speak directly into your heart:

I know your frailty
    Weakness
    Efforts
    Failures
    Your turning toward and away.
You are secure.
I am not waiting for your wholeness
    Completeness
    Perfection
I want you as you are.

Come into my arms.
Rest your head on My shoulder
Feel my warmth and security.
It is yours, belongs to you.
Forever.

I embrace you as you are now.
I rejoice over you now.
I delight in you now.
    Not some future you.
Come as you are.
    No resistance
    No hesitation
    No anxiety
    No fear
    Total acceptance
    Total love
    No "if"
    No "but"
You are all I want.
Doubts will come—they are part of growth
    As is fear
But you have courage to keep on.
You have faltered
    Misstepped
    Fallen.
Yet you kept on—you didn't quit.
That makes Me glad
    Smile
    Laugh with joy.

Relax in Me
      My embrace of you
      My love for you
      My joy in you.

I love you desperately.

The Comfort of His Mercies

Father of mercies and God of all comfort;
who comforts us in all our affliction
so that we may be able to comfort . . .
2 Corinthians 1:3–4

I LOVE THE IMAGE EVOKED by the phrase "Father of mercies." A father is (supposed to be) a protector, provider, leader, an example. A father is kind and tender. A father listens, dries tears, holds, and gives all that he has to take care of his child.

God is the perfect Father. He is all of the above and more. Mercy, giving grace instead of judgment, originates in God. We all deserve judgment and condemnation for our sin. But God applied mercy. We don't deserve it, but He gives it freely and liberally so that we don't have to live under that burden. He has set us free. That is a comfort.

The apostle Paul calls God the "God of all comfort." What comforts you when you are in need? Your mother's home cooking? A special place? Chocolate-chip cookies? The arms of a loved one? God is comfort. That is part of His nature. He is not stingy with His comfort. He gives it all. He provides tender comfort for whatever you are facing.

One of the great comforts is that our suffering, loss, and difficulty are not for naught—there is purpose in them. God brings us through trials so that we may be of use in another's life and so that we may pass along the comfort He gave to us. I certainly have found that true in my own life. When I was struggling with my husband's infidelity many years ago, my child's drug use, another's eating disorder, another's teen pregnancies, and my own depression, I never dreamed that my story would bring comfort and hope to thousands. God took all that mess and made it useful. And what greater comfort is there than to know we have made a difference in someone else's life?

Take a moment and think about a time when you needed comfort. What provided it for you? Now think of someone you know who needs comforting. Ask God to help you reach out appropriately and sensitively to that person—perhaps using the very thing God used in your life. Then make a plan to follow through with it.

Comforting Father,
Thank You for being the source of mercy and comfort. Thank You for showing me mercy when I deserved condemnation. Thank You for comforting me when I am undone. And for telling me that it isn't in vain—You have a purpose for me in the life of another who may be going through much the same thing as I have. Open my eyes to see the need for comfort around me. Amen.

The Comfort of His Greatness

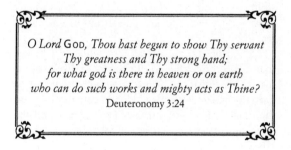

*O Lord GOD, Thou hast begun to show Thy servant
Thy greatness and Thy strong hand;
for what god is there in heaven or on earth
who can do such works and mighty acts as Thine?*
Deuteronomy 3:24

GOD IS A GREAT God. All His attributes are
superlatives.

Yet how many of us live as if God were not
great? Perhaps we find His greatness too hard to
comprehend, and it frightens us. We do not understand Him, so we have made Him small to fit our
thinking and way of living. We whittle Him down to
be manageable. But God cannot be "managed."

It is His very greatness that brings us comfort. I
don't want to trust a god who isn't impressive. I need
Him to be great. When facing decisions for my life, I

want to be able to tap into His great plans for my life. I want to call on His great wisdom. I want to immerse myself in His great peace. When facing illness or tragedy, I want to feel His great compassion and faithfulness. I want to know His great hope and help. When feeling alone or forgotten, I want to know His great presence, His great tenderness, His great understanding. When I am worn out, I need His great ability to sustain me. When I sin, I want to know His great forgiveness and great redemption and great restoration.

Yes, I need a great God. One who is far bigger than I can comprehend but chooses to dwell within me by His Spirit. As believers, we are privileged to have this great, awesome God who cares about even the smallest details of our lives. He listens to and answers our prayers. When we call for help, He is there. His greatness is our comfort.

Take a moment and choose one attribute of God that you need today. You can choose one from those mentioned above or think of another one. Think about how it applies to your life today. Ask God to make it real to you in your situation, and begin to apply it for yourself.

Great heavenly Father,
Thank You that You are a great God. I confess that
often I have made You smaller to fit into my plans
and thinking. Forgive me. I need your greatness to
touch my smallness. Today I need Your great
wisdom as I confront a major decision. You have
great plans for my life, and I need to know which
decision fits into Your plan and purpose for me.
I thank You now for answering my prayer. Amen.

His Comfort Will Sustain You

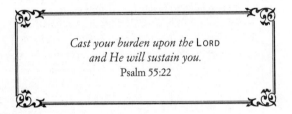

Cast your burden upon the LORD
and He will sustain you.
Psalm 55:22

THE MESSAGE PARAPHRASES THE above verse as, "Pile your troubles on God's shoulders—he'll carry your load, he'll help you out." So go ahead. Pile it on. Pause right now and verbalize to God all the woes, big and small, that are burdening you today. Pile it on His shoulders. When I am feeling particularly stressed and I talk to God, I don't use fancy prayers. I don't make it flowery and spiritual. I just let it out. Tell Him how I feel—get it off my chest. He doesn't mind honesty—He knows what you are thinking and feeling anyway.

Are you ready now to take Him at His word? He

will help you. Yes, really. Oh, the situation may not change before your eyes. Your dinner may still be burned, your money still tight, your tire flat and in need of repair, the kids will argue, and you'll have to call the plumber. The spouse who walked out may not come back. The teenager you've been praying for may still defy your authority and challenge you at every turn. The diagnosis you just got may not change. Or maybe it will. Sometimes God does sweep in and dramatically change our circumstances, and sometimes He does not. Only God knows what tomorrow holds. You, however, do know who holds tomorrow. And that same God will hold you through tomorrow.

God doesn't promise to take us out of the trials of life, He promises to sustain us through them. To sustain means to strengthen, to support, to nourish. He will do all of that—for certain. His strength is at your disposal. He does support you. He will nourish you in all the ways that you need. He sustains you.

Take a moment and notice how your body is working right now. Breathe deeply, feel your pulse, stretch your muscles, swallow. As sure as the next beat of your heart, so sure is God's sustaining comfort. Tomorrow will come. God will show you the next right step. Cast your burdens on Him and let Him handle them. He will not only sustain you but will give you wisdom and guidance.

Dear heavenly Sustainer,
I am stressed to the max. I want to scream. I am
tired of life, and I need Your help. I am going to
pile my troubles onto Your shoulders and let You
carry them while I take a hot bath. Thank You for
Your promise to sustain me during this stressful
time. Help me to calm down and see things more
clearly. Thank You. Amen.

The Comfort of His Invitation

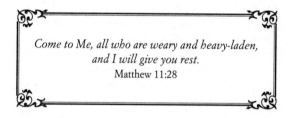

*Come to Me, all who are weary and heavy-laden,
and I will give you rest.*
Matthew 11:28

Isn't it nice to get an invitation? Someone wants us. We are included. When I get an invitation, one of the first things I ask myself is, do I have the right thing to wear? I wonder who the other guests will be. Will I fit in?

Read this verse and look at the guest list. The weary. The heavy laden. The drained. The worn out. The disillusioned. The disappointed. The cynical. Those who need comfort. Not a very fancy crowd. But I fit in!

Well, guess what? You are on the invitation list too! And you need not worry about the right thing to wear. It is come just as you are. Come with your weariness, disillusionment, cynicism. You are welcome. All are welcome.

And look who is issuing the invitation. Jesus. He wants you and me. He knows the effects of the fallen world on us. He knows what it is to be stressed and weary. He knows and understands. He does not condemn. Just the opposite. He invites us to come to find rest, comfort, and inner peace. Don't we long for that? He will give that to us when we come. He says, "I *will* give you rest." It is a promise. The rest He gives is the rest we desperately long for—rest for our souls. Comfort for day-to-day living. Spiritual rest.

It is a simple and profound invitation. "Come." No conditions except your need. I am ready. Are you?

Take a moment and hear His personal invitation to you. "Come [insert your own name]_____." Yield to His graciousness and love. Picture Jesus standing in front of you with His arms open wide. Go to Him. Collapse into His arms. Let Him hold you, and feel the weariness, disillusionment, and cynicism drain from you. Drop your burdens at His feet. Feel His rest and comfort begin to flow into you. Say yes to His invitation.

Heavenly Burden Lifter,
I come to You, weary with life. Burdened. Disillu-
sioned. Cynical. But You said to come, so here I
am. I want what You are offering—rest and com-
fort. I am desperate for rest. The rest only You can
give that will provide inner peace. I now exchange
my burden for Your peace and comfort. Thank
You. Amen.

Day 30

The Comfort of His Reassurance

O taste and see that the LORD is good;
how blessed is the man who takes refuge in Him!
Psalm 34:8

I LIKE TO COOK—ESPECIALLY WHEN there is someone to enjoy the results. As I read this verse, I ask why the verse was not phrased *see*, then *taste*? One thing that has always been an important part of cooking is the presentation, so the plate of food looks appealing and appetizing. A lot of effort goes into the presentation. Food slopped on a plate loses something—even if it is a fabulous recipe, we aren't attracted to it because of poor presentation.

So back to "taste and see." When I was young and Mother served a new dish I didn't want to eat, she always told me, "Take at least one bite, and if you don't like it, you don't have to eat it." She wanted me to taste it so that I would find out how delicious it was. Tasting involves our senses: taste, smell, vision—we ingest the food—take it into us. It becomes part of us. As we taste, our eyes are opened to its delights.

When we are undone by life's trials, often there is a bitter taste in our mouths. Sorrow leaves us empty. God, through the psalmist, invites us to taste Him: His delicacies of comfort, unconditional love, grace, forgiveness . . . Once we have tasted, we know how good He truly is. He takes away the bitter taste left by the things that have wounded us, hardened us, made us cynical. He fills up the empty places left by loss and sorrow. He comes into our lives with His character and begins to transform us according to His good plan for us.

The verse adds, "How blessed is the man who takes refuge in Him!" Yes, when life undoes us, we need a place to go to find healing and wholeness once again. He is that place. He is our refuge and shelter from the storm.

Taste and see today.

Take a moment and think of what has you undone. What aspect of God's character do you need to taste in order to see His goodness? Do you need to know His faithfulness? His compassion and mercy? His strength? His nearness? His protection? Taste of it. Take it in and make it a part of you today. You will find in Him healing and wholeness.

Comforting Father,
Life has left me undone and reeling. I confess that I
feel bitter and angry—even with You. It actually
feels good, but I know it is harmful for me to stay
here. You invite me to taste of Your character and
see that it is good. So by faith I ask You to remove
the bitterness, anger, and emptiness and fill me up
with Your nature so that I may grow into the per-
son You planned for me to be. Thank You. Amen.

Day 31

The Comfort of His Closeness

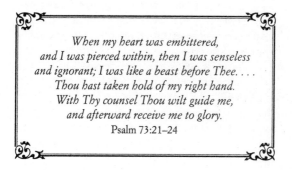

When my heart was embittered,
and I was pierced within, then I was senseless
and ignorant; I was like a beast before Thee. . . .
Thou hast taken hold of my right hand.
With Thy counsel Thou wilt guide me,
and afterward receive me to glory.
Psalm 73:21–24

HAVE YOU EVER BEEN in anguish and felt like the psalmist was feeling? Bitter? Wounded? Those emotions take over our minds, tainting all that we do, think, say—we become as the psalmist says "senseless and ignorant." We cannot hear reason and counsel. We act out of impulse—we'll do anything to stop the pain we feel. We lash out at those we hold most dear. We do, indeed, act beastly. We act beastly before God as well.

It is as if we are saying, "I know You are supposed to be a good and wise and merciful God, but right now the reality I am facing doesn't match up with that, and I cannot reconcile Your nature with what I am experiencing and seeing." God lets us go through such experiences. Believe it or not, it strengthens our relationship with Him, if we let it. It is our choice. Elsewhere the psalmist tells us, "Before I was afflicted I went astray, but now I keep Thy word" (Psalm 119:67). We can allow our trials to harden us, becoming bitter, or soften us, making us more like Jesus.

God knows it is hard. He doesn't sugarcoat it. But it has purpose. Our anguish has a purpose for our lives. I find that a comfort. It isn't just by chance—there is a plan. God doesn't leave us alone to struggle on the best way we can. He takes our right hand. To do that, He has to be nearby—by our side. I don't know about you, but when someone takes my hand, I turn to look at the person. To see who it is, what she wants. When God takes our hands, let us look to Him and see what He wants. He promises to guide us through the darkness and grief. And will lead us to glory. That's where I want to go. That is something for which to be thankful.

Take a moment and think about how you are reacting to the trial in your life today. Now put your right hand in your lap, palm up. Release the struggle to God, and feel His hand grasp yours. He is right there with you, beside you. As hard as it may be, thank Him for working in your life, and ask Him to

help you become more aware of His presence in your
life.

Heavenly Father,
I confess that I have acted, am acting, beastly
in the struggle I am facing. I do not have the re-
sources I need to handle this. I am angry and frus-
trated and hurting. But by faith I release it all to
You now and ask that You take my hand and guide
me by Your Spirit. Help me to trust You even when
I have questions. Thank You for loving me and
walking with me. Amen.

The Comfort of His Tenderness

> *He shall feed his flock like a shepherd:*
> *he shall gather the lambs with his arm,*
> *and carry them in his bosom,*
> *and shall gently lead those that are with young.*
> Isaiah 40:11 (KJV)

SO OFTEN PEOPLE SEE God as harsh, distant, and hard to please. This verse is such a picture of God's tenderness and closeness. It pictures God as a shepherd. A shepherd is one who guards and protects; he feeds and tends to the sheep when they are sick or troubled; he corrects when they wander off; he safely leads them; and if one gets lost, he goes to find it. A good shepherd knows what his sheep need.

As a young girl, I traveled with my family to the Holy Land. I remember the sheep in the fields and in the towns, blocking traffic. We noticed that some of the sheep had a red mark painted on their wool, and my mother asked what it was. She was told by our guide that the man tending the flock was not the shepherd but a hireling, and he did not know the sheep, whereas the shepherd had no need to mark his sheep, for he knew the ones that were his—he had a relationship with each one. And the sheep knew his voice. If they became agitated, he would talk to them, and they would settle down. We noticed that the sheep pens had no gates, and when we inquired as to why, the guide told us that at night the shepherd would place himself across the entry so that nothing could get by him to hurt his sheep.

Jesus calls Himself the Good Shepherd. He knows us. He tends us, cares for us, and supplies our needs. "The LORD is my shepherd, I shall not want" (Psalm 23:1). And He corrects and disciplines us as a father would his child, lovingly, gently. When we are tired or sick or in special need, He gathers us in His arms and carries us in His embrace. Close. Intimate. Protected. And He gently leads those who are caring for the young ones. He knows how exhausting caring for little ones can be—the sleepless nights, the constant demands, the mounds of laundry—so there is special attention given to them. He knows, and He is particularly gentle with those with young. All young parents find comfort here!

God is tender with us. He is not harsh. He is not distant. He knows what your needs are, and He is caring for you even as you read this.

Take a moment and make a list of how God has

taken care of your needs this week. Perhaps you got a call you were waiting for or a friend came by to drop off a casserole. Maybe you were able to get an extra hour of sleep or a bill got paid. Take time to recognize how He takes care of you and blesses your life.

Tender Father,
Thank You for how You gently and tenderly care
for me. I often only see my needs and do not stop
to look for Your blessings. Forgive me. Please open
my eyes to see Your fingerprints in my life. Thank
You. Amen.

part five

Encounter His Power

His Power Is Sufficient

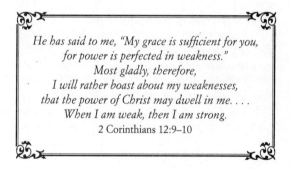

*He has said to me, "My grace is sufficient for you,
for power is perfected in weakness."
Most gladly, therefore,
I will rather boast about my weaknesses,
that the power of Christ may dwell in me. . . .
When I am weak, then I am strong.*
2 Corinthians 12:9–10

WE ARE A CULTURE that admires power. The apostle Paul knew about power—he had walked in the corridors of the powerful and influential. However, God's power prefers human weakness. Paul's life changed when God called him from being a leader in the persecution of the early church to being a servant of the very church he had tried to destroy. Many times Paul faced situations over which he had no control (see 2 Corinthians 11:25).

In that chapter Paul implored God to remove some affliction that Satan had used to harass him, making his life that much harder. Three times Paul asked God to take it away. Now, you might expect God to answer the apostle Paul affirmatively, *Of course, Paul. I want to free you of this so you will be even more powerful and effective for Me.* Isn't that the way we want God to answer us? To take away the problem, to remove the difficult person, to heal the illness, to fill our bank account, return the prodigal?

Look at the answer Paul got from God. It shows that God heard Paul's prayers, was aware of the problem, but had a greater purpose than Paul's relief in mind. God said, "My grace is sufficient for you, for power is perfected in weakness." Paul was right where God wanted him to be. Powerless. Paul had to depend on God exclusively—not on his connections, not his intellect, not his influence. Only on God.

Paul accepted God's answer and said, "I am well content with weaknesses, with insults, with distresses, with persecutions, with difficulties for Christ's sake; for when I am weak, then I am strong." What a remarkable attitude! No whining. No pouting or anger. No self-focus. Paul simply yielded himself to God's purposes so that God's power would shine through him.

Take a moment. What is your weakness—the thing that you feel hinders you? Remember other times when you felt weak and helpless. What did God do? Choose to yield your weakness to Him so that He might reveal His glory through the very thing you struggle against.

Great and strong God,
I confess that I like to feel in control. I don't like to
feel weak. Right now I do—I have no power
over_____. Help me to yield to Your purpose in
this situation, step back, and let You work out Your
purpose for Your glory. Thank You. Amen.

His Power Is Your Source

> *The LORD is my strength and song,*
> *and He has become my salvation.*
> Exodus 15:2

THIS SCRIPTURE IS POSTED on my bathroom mirror. It actually came printed on the front of my church newsletter a couple of years ago when I was going through a difficult time. It was just the message I needed, so I cut it out and taped it to my mirror. It is still there. It is still the message I need.

The Hebrews were celebrating after being delivered from the Egyptians. God had miraculously intervened on their behalf. And now they are all out celebrating. I have been told that this verse is the first mention of singing in the Bible. They sing of God being highly exalted, that He is victorious.

God delivered them. They recognize His deliverance. They praise Him. Can you imagine the joy they felt? The relief? The freedom? That which had kept them awake at night with worry. That which had been the topic of conversation in every tent and at every council meeting. That which they feared so greatly. Now gone. Wiped out by God's powerful hand.

They rejoice in His strength and know He is their salvation. That's the bottom line for us today. When I posted that verse on my bathroom mirror, I was feeling pursued by those far more powerful than I. The only One I could rely on was God. I needed His strength to get me through—I had run out of my resources. I needed His intervention in my heart.

Each day I would read that verse and find the strength I needed to get through. At first it was hard to praise Him with a hurting heart, but I would remember His character and praise Him for Himself. I didn't have to manufacture the song—He is the song. I didn't have to produce the strength—He is the strength. And that becomes our salvation—the way to heal heartache.

Take a moment to reread that verse. Let the truth of it sink in. Your circumstances may have drained you of strength and song, but He will give you Himself. Choose to praise Him for His strength, and ask Him to give you a new song in your heart—His song.

God of strength and song,
My heart is hurting. I am drained of strength and
have lost any song in my heart. I choose now to
take on Your strength and song, knowing You are
my salvation. I praise You. Amen.

His Power Is Infinite

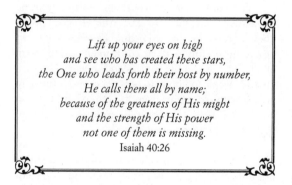

*Lift up your eyes on high
and see who has created these stars,
the One who leads forth their host by number,
He calls them all by name;
because of the greatness of His might
and the strength of His power
not one of them is missing.*
Isaiah 40:26

WHAT A WONDERFUL PICTURE of God's power seen in creation! We are invited to look into the night sky to see God.

A couple of years ago a friend and I went up to the Blue Ridge Parkway near my home to watch a meteor shower. It was a crisp, clear night, and we lay on our backs looking into the night sky. Away from light pollution of the city, we could see the countless stars. An occasional satellite or plane would float across the sky. But so many stars—there was no way to see them all, much less count them.

God has names for them all! What kind of mind can do that—can grasp the infinite? Only God's. The greatness of His authority and the strength of His command is the reason they all hold together. He is supreme over all creation.

This could make us feel small and insignificant. But actually quite the opposite is true. His great power doesn't keep Him isolated behind heavenly walls. His power draws Him to us. He chose to take on the form of an infant to identify with us and show us His great love. He wants to know us, personally and intimately. He chose to redeem us from the grip of sin. He is so powerful that by His death He conquered death so that we might have eternal life.

Take a moment tonight and look up into the sky. Think of the greatness of our God—the power that not only created but sustains all of creation—including you. God sees you. You are of great significance to God. He has called you by name to be His very own. Have you made Him your own by giving control of your life to Him as your Creator, Sustainer, and Savior?

Overwhelming God,
You do reveal Yourself through nature. It is won-
derful to see. I confess that all too often I am so
caught up in the busyness of life that I fail to no-
tice Your fingerprints not only in nature but in
my life. Forgive me. Thank You that your great
power did not keep You from me, but You chose
me by name to be Your own child. I love You.
Amen.

His Power Is Awesome

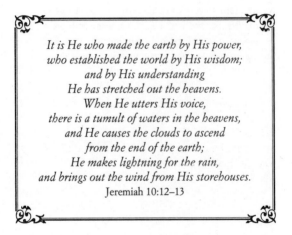

It is He who made the earth by His power,
who established the world by His wisdom;
and by His understanding
He has stretched out the heavens.
When He utters His voice,
there is a tumult of waters in the heavens,
and He causes the clouds to ascend
from the end of the earth;
He makes lightning for the rain,
and brings out the wind from His storehouses.
Jeremiah 10:12–13

W HAT DOES THIS PASSAGE tell us about God? It tells us that He has power and wisdom and understanding. He uses them to make, establish, and stretch out our universe. He has a voice, and He speaks. And when He speaks, things happen in the universe and nature. He is in control of it all. That is the God we have—an awesome God.

When we are feeling helpless and powerless, we know the One who has all power and all authority. He reigns over all kingdoms and powers. After the terrorist attack in New York City and Washington, D.C., in 2001, my mother used to say, "God's throne was not shaken, and He still sits on the throne." That was comforting. It still is.

You may feel as if your life has been blown apart by illness, death, financial loss, betrayal, or a host of things. Life is out of control and seems to be crashing down around you. You wonder where God is in all of this and if He even cares. Let me assure you that His power, wisdom, and understanding are directed your way. You may not feel Him or see Him, but He is there. He is establishing His plan for your life. Sometimes He has to stretch us, and that can be painful. Scripture tells us He has a plan for our wholeness. He will give us a hope and a future (see Jeremiah 29:11). Claim that promise as your own, and trust your powerful God to accomplish His plan for you.

Take a moment and remember another time when you felt things were out of control. You felt powerless. What happened? How did God help you? How did God reveal His plans for you then? Expect Him to establish His good plan in this thing that has you fearful.

Awesome God,
I confess I am feeling helpless and powerless. I am
finding it difficult to trust You during this time.
Please help me. I thank You for the ways You have
revealed Your power before. I want to know Your
power, wisdom, and understanding in my current
situation. I need to hear Your voice. Please open
my eyes to see You. Thank You. Amen.

His Power Is Incomparable

> *Who is like Thee among the gods, O LORD?*
> *Who is like Thee, majestic in holiness, awesome in*
> *praises, working wonders?*
> Exodus 15:11

WE DON'T USUALLY THINK that we live in a culture that serves multiple gods. But perhaps we do. I am not talking about multiple religions—we do live amongst people of various faiths. But multiple gods? What takes God's place in your life? A good way to determine what god we serve is to ask ourselves: *What do I think about most? What do I spend most of my time doing? Where do I spend most of my money? Where does most of my energy go?*

We can make almost anything into a god—money, status, food, sex, a relationship. We use these things to try to comfort, stabilize, bring joy, fulfill, provide a measure of peace. And perhaps for a time they may do that, but none can give any lasting satisfaction. There is the need for more—these things operate on the law of diminishing returns. There is always an empty, unsettled place. The one true God, Jehovah, is the only One who brings satisfaction and true fulfillment in life.

Moses tells us in the above passage that Jehovah is incomparable. There is no god like Him in majestic holiness—unmatched purity. In heaven the living creatures that surround His throne do not cease to cry, "Holy, Holy, Holy." He is awesome in praises—breathtaking in superlatives. Again, in heaven the elders that surround the throne say, "Worthy art Thou, our Lord and our God, to receive glory and honor and power; for Thou didst create all things, and because of Thy will they existed, and were created" (Revelation 4:11). He works wonders—"Things which eye has not seen and ear has not heard, and which have not entered the heart of man, all that God has prepared for those who love Him" (1 Corinthians 2:9). He is incomparable, unmatched. And He wants to be in relationship with you.

Take a moment to praise God for His matchless holiness. Picture the beauty of heaven's throne room—the colors of jasper (reddish brown) and sardius (red); a rainbow surrounding the throne; emeralds, white garments, and golden crowns. Lightning flashes and thunder crashes. Lamps of fire. A crystal sea in front of the throne. Those around the throne worshipping in ceaseless praise. And on the throne sits the eternal God. What glory! Yes, we have an incomparable God who is also our heavenly Father. Take no substitute.

Incomparable and holy Father,
I worship You now. Thank You that there is no
other God but You. Thank You that You are holy
and matchless and that You care about me. For-
give me for making You too small, taking You for
granted. Enlarge my vision of You. Thank You for
loving me. Amen.

His Power Is Incomprehensible

> *Oh, the depth of the riches*
> *both of the wisdom and knowledge of God!*
> *How unsearchable are His judgments*
> *and unfathomable His ways!*
> Romans 11:33

A S FINITE HUMAN BEINGS, we cannot understand the infinite mind and ways of God. He is beyond our ability to comprehend. In this verse the apostle Paul exclaims the incomprehensibility of God. But Paul tells us that the wisdom and knowledge of God is rich. Not only rich, but deeply rich. In other words, it is worth the effort to seek out His wisdom and knowledge. He is worth knowing. He has told us that if we seek Him with all of our hearts, we will find Him (see Jeremiah 29:13).

We like to understand or try to figure things

out—how they are made, how they work, why they do what they do. That helps us to feel comfortable and gives us a sense of control. However, God cannot be put in a box. If He could, then He wouldn't be much of a God—He would be finite just like us. God is so much more. He has shown Himself. Oh, that we had the eyes to see! How does God reveal Himself to us?

God has revealed Himself to us through the Scriptures, showing us how He deals with humans—justly, with wisdom, patience, and gentleness. He's left His fingerprints in nature—in the majesty of the alpine peaks, the delicacy of a butterfly wing, the joy of a baby's giggle. We see His work in the lives of other people as they are changed by His grace in their lives from sinners to saints.

Beyond what we see and feel, God also asks us to trust. Trust His character. When it is dark and we cannot see ahead, when we are in pain with no relief, when our hearts are breaking, when we are lost and cannot find our way, when we are tired and confused, we drill down to His character. And look up—see Him in all that is around you, and praise Him that He is bigger than your finite mind can comprehend, because that means He is big enough to handle your situation.

Take a moment to thank God for the fact that you cannot comprehend Him. That He is more wonderful, more amazing, more delightful, more mighty, more preeminent, more everything than you can imagine. Let worship well up in your heart and begin to praise God for His bigness in your own life today.

Incomprehensible God,
Thank You for all that You are. I need a big God,
one who fills the universe but fits in my heart.
Reveal Yourself to me in nature around me, in the
Scriptures, and in people's changed lives. I want to
know more about You and Your ways and wisdom.
Help me to trust You even when I don't under-
stand. Thank You. Amen.

His Power Is Unchanging

> *"My thoughts are not your thoughts,*
> *neither are your ways My ways," declares the LORD.*
> *"For as the heavens are higher than the earth,*
> *so are My ways higher than your ways,*
> *and My thoughts than Your thoughts."*
> Isaiah 55:8–9

WHO OF US HAS not tried to figure out how God works? When tragedy strikes, we try to come up with a reason. We have formulas and pat answers that we spout too readily. We think He should behave as we might, and when He doesn't, we wonder why He does what He does. His ways are quite different from ours. We cannot reason our way to understand God. Scripture says, "How unsearchable are his judgments, and his ways past finding out! For who hath known the mind of the Lord?" (Romans 11:33–34 KJV).

We cannot know the mind of the Lord. Job struggled to understand God's ways after he lost everything: his children, his servants, livestock, wealth, his house, and his health. The few friends he had left had lots of "reasoned" answers for a deeply wounded Job. They declared they knew God's ways. They had formulas and pat answers. In the end, God rebuked them. Job said we only know the "fringes of His ways" (Job 26:14) and concluded, "Thou canst do all things, and . . . no purpose of Thine can be thwarted" (Job 42:2).

Job focused on the character of God. After all his devastating loss, we are told, "He fell to the ground and worshiped. And he said, 'Naked I came from my mother's womb, and naked I shall return there. The LORD gave and the LORD has taken away. Blessed be the name of the LORD.' Through all this Job did not sin nor did he blame God" (Job 1:20–22).

When we find ourselves powerless and weak, out of control, and asking why, we must remember God's character as Job did. As difficult as it may be, let us take the time to worship God and His unchanging character. He loves us. He knows what is best for us. Can we trust Him? Even when we are in the dark? When we are suffering? Job did.

Take a moment and choose to worship. I would suggest that if you can, get on your knees and bow before Him. You can tell Him you do not understand His ways but you understand from Scripture and those whose lives are told in Scripture that He is in control, has your best interests in His plan for you, and that you trust His character absolutely. Tell Him you trust Him and His ways even though you do not understand.

Holy God,
I know I don't understand Your ways. I confess
that I do try to figure things out on my own, but,
Lord, You would rather have me simply trust You
and Your character. I know Your ways are much
better than mine. I do believe; help my unbelief.
Thank You. Amen.

His Power Is Glorious

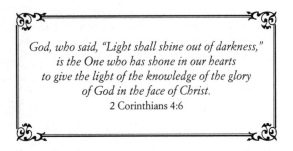

God, who said, "Light shall shine out of darkness,"
is the One who has shone in our hearts
to give the light of the knowledge of the glory
of God in the face of Christ.
2 Corinthians 4:6

I LOVE THIS VERSE! THE creator God who said, "'Let there be light'; and there was light" (Genesis 1:3), has brought light into our lives, into our hearts. No longer do we have to live in the dark. The God of the universe, Creator of all things, wants to illumine our minds so that we can know His glory. That is amazing! God wanted to put a human face on His glory—the face of Jesus. All of His glory is encapsulated in Jesus' face.

The Bible never reveals what Jesus looked like. Isaiah's prophecy does tell us that, "He has no stately form or majesty that we should look upon Him, nor appearance that we should be attracted to Him" (Isaiah 53:2). He wouldn't make the cover of *People* magazine! We had Sunday-school images of Him that we may still hold in our minds, but they were usually rather bland and tame. Jesus was anything but tame! He was the Creator. He caused the wind and waves to obey Him. He cast out demons. He healed the sick and blind. As a carpenter, He would be strong with rough hands. He threw the money changers out of the temple. He confounded religious leaders and scholars. No, He was not tame. God is not tame and cannot be tamed.

The glory of God is revealed in Jesus' face. His face must have been kind and welcoming. His eyes, clear and gentle. No doubt they twinkled. His smile, tender. His laughter, easy and contagious. He was approachable and winsome—not off-putting. Children were drawn to Him, and He gathered them around Him. But His face also would show grief. Grief for the bondage people were in—He could see into the heart of man. It would reveal the sorrow of a burden bearer. And it would reveal hope. He knew He brought good news, redemption for all mankind. He knew the heart of God—He was the heart of God. The glory of God is revealed in the face of Jesus.

Take a moment and imagine Jesus' face. He is smiling at you with love. Smile back! How does it feel? Enjoy the moment.

Glorious God,
Thank You for revealing Your glory in the face of
Jesus. Help me to see it more clearly each day and
enjoy You. And may I live in such a way that You
are revealed in my life. Thank You for loving me.
Amen.

part six

Receive His Help

The Help of His Stability

*The Helper, the Holy Spirit,
whom the Father will send in My name,
He will teach you all things,
and bring to your remembrance all that I said to you.*
John 14:26

GOD KNOWS WE NEED help. And before we were even aware of our need, He made provision for us. The character of God is to help, and the Holy Spirit is the agent. When we invite Jesus to be our Savior, the Holy Spirit takes up residence in our lives at that very moment. His presence is to help and empower us to live as God wants us to. We cannot do it on our own. "For it is God who is at work in you, both to will and to work for His good pleasure" (Philippians 2:13).

We see in the above passage that another name

for the Holy Spirit is "Helper." When we are in need of help, desperate need of help, and we don't even know how to pray, He helps us. "The Spirit also helps our weakness; for we do not know how to pray as we should, but the Spirit Himself intercedes for us with groanings too deep for words" (Romans 8:26). Have you been in such a place? Not knowing how to pray? You can't even focus your mind to form thoughts, much less words.

You desperately need help and yet cannot seem to even ask for it. God understands. So He has provided us with help. That scripture goes on to tell us, "And He who searches the hearts knows what the mind of the Spirit is, because He intercedes for the saints according to the will of God" (v. 27). The Holy Spirit interprets our inarticulate efforts so that they align with God's will for us. And it is God who knows what is best for us and our loved ones.

Take a moment. What is heavy on your heart today? Have you run out of options? Maybe your child is in trouble. Your marriage is ending. You have received a terrible diagnosis. You are numb. Just be still and know that the Holy Spirit hears your heart-ache-hurting groans, interpreting them and taking them right into God's throne room where they get God's full attention. You are not alone. You have a Helper right with you all the time.

Holy Spirit,
Thank You for being my helper. I am hurting too
deeply to tell You what I feel, much less think.
Please interpret this deep grief, and take it to God.
Thank You. Amen.

The Help of His Authenticity

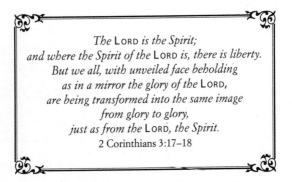

The LORD is the Spirit;
and where the Spirit of the LORD is, there is liberty.
But we all, with unveiled face beholding
as in a mirror the glory of the LORD,
are being transformed into the same image
from glory to glory,
just as from the LORD, the Spirit.
2 Corinthians 3:17–18

IT IS INTERESTING TO me that the apostle Paul uses these two verses together. He talks about liberty but then about being transformed. What does that mean? How does that work?

How many times have I asked God to help me know Him better? Yet so many times when my heart is heavy or I am afraid, I put on my happy face and tell everyone, "I'm fine." I want to hide my real self. If people truly knew what was going on in my life, they might be disappointed in me or, worse, reject me. I may be ready to scream, but I act like I have everything under control. I need help, but I keep up the pretense. That is probably true of all of us.

That is not what God wants for us. He has provided us help in the form of liberty—freedom. Freedom from pretense. Freedom to be authentic. Freedom to believe that God is who He says He is! If we don't have freedom and are held captive by rules that we feel we must keep in order to please God, or are bound by our fears and anxieties, or compelled to keep up appearances, that is not where God is. His Spirit is one of liberty. When we are at liberty, we ourselves are helped and free to help others.

Taking off the masks makes us vulnerable. We don't want to be vulnerable. We could get hurt. But when we take off our masks we can see God more clearly. He doesn't wear a mask. God wants to be seen and known by free people. Jesus died so that we might experience freedom and authenticity.

As we behold Him in our own authenticity, our own vulnerability, we are transformed by the glory of God to be like Him. We begin to reflect Him. God can use you more effectively when you are free. When you are authentic, you reflect more of who He is and become more like Him.

Take a moment to think about the mask you tend to wear. Does it help you know God better?

Other people? Yourself? Do you want to reflect God's glory? Are you willing to let the mask go? To be authentic? There is freedom there.

God of freedom and liberty,
I confess that too often I hide behind a "pretty"
mask. But You see through it. You want to give me
the freedom to be all that You want me to be. You
want me to be authentic so I will reflect Your glory.
Help me to let go of the pretense. Thank You.
Amen.

The Help of His Grace

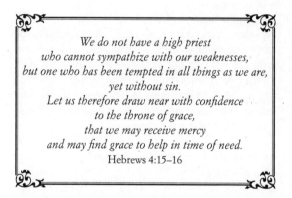

*We do not have a high priest
who cannot sympathize with our weaknesses,
but one who has been tempted in all things as we are,
yet without sin.
Let us therefore draw near with confidence
to the throne of grace,
that we may receive mercy
and may find grace to help in time of need.*
Hebrews 4:15–16

THIS HAS TO BE one of my favorite Bible verses. It reveals God's heart toward us. We can have confidence as we approach the throne of grace, because the One who sits there is our loving heavenly Father. We have nothing to fear. Imagine you have broken the law and must stand before a judge. You worry about it for weeks ahead of time. You are anxious and very nervous. Finally the hour arrives, and as you are ushered into the courtroom, you are intimidated until you look up and see, not a judge but your father. Your fear is erased. He tells you that he is a better judge because he has experienced what you have experienced. He gently asks that you tell him what you need, and when you confess, unburden yourself, he says, *Of course I'll help you. You are my child. I love you.*

God is telling us in these two verses that He has experienced life as we have—with all its temptations, trials, and disappointments. And because He has, He sympathizes with our weaknesses. He understands. We can go to Him boldly, not arrogantly, not presumptuously, but with every one of our needs—no matter how small or how big or how often. He is there to help us in time of need.

He would much rather we come to Him than try to fix things in our own strength and our own way. When we do, we mess it up—make it worse. No. He invites us to come to Him first. He is ready to help us—every time. "He Himself has said, 'I will never desert you, nor will I ever forsake you,' so that we confidently say, 'The Lord is my helper, I will not be afraid'" (Hebrews 13:5–6).

Take a moment and imagine the courtroom scene with you in it. Instead of feeling intimidated or anxious, imagine coming in with confidence and assurance that you will find the grace and help you need because your Father is the One who sits on the throne. Tell Him your need—open your heart to Him. Then leave it with Him.

Sympathetic Father,
I am glad that you experienced life as I do and un-
derstand the hardships of life. Thank you that You
invite me to come to You boldly. I come now bur-
dened by my sin of_____. I seem to succumb to it
so often. But I come to You for grace and mercy.
Please forgive me and help me. Thank You for
being my Helper who never will desert me no
matter how often I come to You for help. Amen.

Day 44

The Help of His Joy

Do not be grieved,
for the joy of the LORD *is your strength.*
Nehemiah 8:10

WHAT DOES JOY HAVE to do with God being our help? What does it have to do with strength? And what is the "joy of the LORD"? God tells us not to be grieved, but instead of telling us it is all going to be okay and work out as we want, He says that His joy is our strength; I was asking for strength, I was asking for relief. Does joy satisfy grief? I need help, not some elusive joy.

What is the "joy of the LORD" anyway? I have thought about that a lot. As a parent of young children, what made me happy, joyful, when it came to my children? Obedience. When my children were young and I created a structure for them, I was de-

lighted when they obeyed and followed the plan.
Disobedience brought discord and unhappiness. It
resulted in discipline and crying. Unhappiness. It
was much easier when they obeyed—when they respected my rules. Obedience in a family helps things
move more smoothly, and it is a parent's delight. I
didn't make rules in order to make my children un-
happy and miserable. My job was not to make them
happy, but to make them good. I made rules to help
them grow and mature into responsible adults.

It is the same in God's family. God delights in
our obedience. It is His joy. And it is wise for us to
obey Him because things will go better for us when
we do follow God's Word. "How blessed is the man
who fears the LORD, who greatly delights in His
commandments" (Psalm 112:1). He has put rules in
place to protect us. Just like lines on a highway are
put there for our protection. Drive your car outside
of them, and disaster could befall you! "He who sins
against me injures himself" (Proverbs 8:36). God's
Word is there to help us mature as Christians. Obedience is a strength, a refuge for us. It helps us. Disobedience can block God's help.

Take a moment and ask yourself what brings
you joy. When was the last time you felt true joy? In
your mind do you relate joy with obedience? Doesn't
life go more smoothly when we are obeying God's
Word? Is there an area of disobedience in your life?
Is it blocking the help you so desperately need? Confess it and ask Him to help you be obedient to His
Word in your life.

God of joy,
Thank You for continuing to work in my life.
Thank you that Your joy, my obedience, is my
strength and refuge. It helps me grow in You, and
that is what I want. Forgive me for going my own
way, being stubborn and disobedient. I know it
blocks Your help for me. I need Your help. Thank
You. Amen.

Day 45

The Help of His Strength

> *The LORD is my strength and my shield;*
> *My heart trusts in Him, and I am helped;*
> *therefore my heart exults, and with my song*
> *I shall thank Him.*
> Psalm 28:7

I CANNOT DO THIS UNPREDICTABLE path called life on my own. I need help—some days more than others. Usually when I need help, I want it right away and I want it the way I think is best. This verse tells me that God is my strength. I have His power within me by the Holy Spirit. When David went out to face Goliath, Goliath taunted him that Israel would send a mere boy to fight for them. David replied, "The battle is the LORD's and He will give you into our hands" (1 Samuel 17:47). David knew and trusted his God. I don't have to fight life's battles in my own strength.

This verse also says that God is my shield, my protector. A shield is a defensive piece of armor—something that covers you and takes the blows of battle. God covers us. We have faith in God's ability to fight the battles for us. He does a much better job. When David went to fight Goliath, he depended on God's protection and strength. As he approached Goliath, David declared, "You come to me with a sword, a spear, and a javelin, but I come to you in the name of the LORD of hosts, the God of the armies of Israel" (1 Samuel 17:45).

David declared that his heart trusted God, and when he placed his trust there, he was helped. His help came from the Lord. It comes back to trust. David didn't trust in his own ability to defeat Goliath. The odds were against David. He found the help he needed when he put his trust in God.

Take a moment. What Goliath do you face today? What overwhelming situation has you frightened? You don't know what to do—it is beyond your ability. Choose to follow David's example. He knew that "the weapons of our warfare are not of the flesh, but divinely powerful for the destruction of fortresses" (2 Corinthians 10:4). Trust Him and find the help you need. And thank Him with a praise song right now.

My Strength and Shield,
I confess that as I look around, I get afraid. How
am I to face tomorrow? Fears multiply and my
strength melts. I feel exposed and vulnerable to
attack. Help me. I turn this battle over to You. I
place my trust in You. I praise You for what You
are going to do. Amen.

The Help of His Blessings

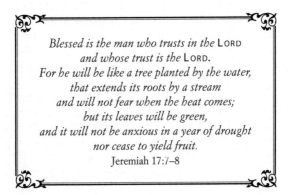

*Blessed is the man who trusts in the L*ORD
*and whose trust is the L*ORD.
For he will be like a tree planted by the water,
that extends its roots by a stream
and will not fear when the heat comes;
but its leaves will be green,
and it will not be anxious in a year of drought
nor cease to yield fruit.
Jeremiah 17:7–8

BEING PLANTED BY THE stream does not necessarily mean we will be watered unless we extend our roots. Roots seek water. The stream's water does not come to them. I had neighbors who piled a ring of mulch around their trees for many years. It looked so pretty and neat. But when they sold the house, the new owners took the mulch away. And do you know what was exposed? Roots. Dry roots. Roots that had been desperate for water had come to the surface—now they were exposed to the elements and disease. The roots had not been allowed to go deep because the water was on the surface.

As Christians we can stand in church, study the Bible, or do community service. We can look good to others, but unless we are extending our roots deep—participating with God's work in our hearts, yielding to the Holy Spirit's promptings, and acting in obedience—we are shallow Christians. Our roots are on the surface, exposed to temptation and sin.

God says that the person who trusts in Him is planted by the deep waters of God's unending source. They are blessed. When the heat comes, they will not fear—they know their source of help. They will still bear fruit, even in drought. Why? Because they chose to extend their roots deep into God's unchanging character.

That does not mean it will be easy. This verse talks of heat and drought. Are you there? The heat has come and you don't think you can stand another minute? Your sin and the accuser have made you think you will never be used again—never bear fruit. The drought has made you dry and brittle. Anxious. Fearful.

Extend your roots deeply into the stream of the Holy Spirit. Jesus called Himself the living water (see John 4:10, 13–14). This is where our help comes from—He will refresh. He will cause fruit to grow—you will not cease to yield fruit. God will produce the fruit—perhaps not as you expected or planned, but you will be fruitful in ways that bring God glory. It will be evident to all that He has done it—not you. He will get the glory.

Take a moment and think about God's fruit in your life. Is there any? Are your roots extended deeply into God's Word? Have you surrounded yourself with people who also want to extend their roots deeply? Tell God that you want your roots to go down deep into Him so that you will not only show life but produce fruit.

Heavenly Father,
I don't want to be a surface Christian who when
the hard times come, wilts. I want my roots to go
deep into You so that I will never cease to grow
and yield fruit. Forgive my wanting to take the
easy way. Help me. Thank You. Amen.

Day 47
___

The Help of His Leadership

> *"Who is among you that fears the LORD,*
> *that obeys the voice of His servant,*
> *that walks in darkness and has no light?*
> *Let him trust in the name of the LORD*
> *and rely on his God."*
> Isaiah 50:10

YOU LOVE GOD. You fear Him in the sense of holding him in awe, honor, and reverence. You study His Word and try to live obediently. You pray regularly and live faithfully. You have had precious times where you felt God was very near. But there are times, perhaps even today, when you feel as if you are in the dark. You don't know which way to go. You keep going back to what you know how to do. But nothing works. You can understand what Job meant when he said, "Behold, I go forward but He is not there, and backward, but I cannot perceive Him; when He acts on the left I cannot behold Him; when He turns to the right, I cannot see Him." (Job 23:8–9a).

You search for answers, but there don't seem to be any. Well-meaning people give answers, but they contradict each other, and things just don't make sense. You are confused. Hurt. Why does God let one of His own go through such bleak times? I don't know the answer to that, but I do know that all God's people go through dark times. And I know it is a time of growth. The deep things of God are taught in difficult times. I don't like that, but I know it to be true in my own life.

My relationship with God deepened greatly when I walked in the darkness of depression, divorce, and my family's resulting problems. During that time I had no idea what God was doing. I just knew I hurt. I was confused—in the dark. All I knew to do was to cling to God and that eventually He would show me what to do. He was working out His will in my tomorrows. He promises, "But He knows the way I take; when He has tried me, I shall come forth as gold" (Job 23:9b).

What do we do when we find ourselves in the dark and confused, running out of resources? Our verse says, "Let him trust in the name of the LORD and rely on his God." Our job is to trust the Lord's name—His name reveals His unchanging character—and "rely on his God."

Take a moment to be still. Do you feel abandoned by God when you need Him the most? Tell

God what you are feeling—be honest with Him. He is listening to you even if you do not sense His presence. Choose to believe that He is right there listening, and He will answer. Picture Him with you. He is there.

Dear God,
I am in the dark. I feel abandoned by You. I am frustrated and want to know You are near. I choose to trust Your name and Your promise that You are near. Please help me to see and recognize You today and tomorrow. Thank You. Amen.

Day 48

The Help of His Deliverance

> *Do not fear or be dismayed*
> *because of this great multitude,*
> *for the battle is not yours but God's.*
> 2 Chronicles 20:15

JEHOSHAPHAT, KING OF JUDAH, was seriously outnumbered. Their enemies were fast approaching and ready for war. Judah was no match for these enemies. Jehoshaphat was afraid. What did he do? We are told, "[He] turned his attention to seek help from the LORD." Jehoshaphat said, "Power and might are in Thy hand so that no one can stand against Thee.... We will ... cry to Thee in our distress, and Thou wilt hear and deliver us" (2 Chronicles 20:3–4, 6, 9). He wasn't telling God what the problem was or what to do about it; He was acknowledging

God's authority and power. He was acknowledging his dependence on God for deliverance.

I don't think I have any human enemies. I am sure there are people who don't like me very much, but I would not call them enemies. I doubt if you do either. I do know that I have an Enemy seeking to destroy me. Satan uses our human frailties that become our enemies if we let him gain a toehold in our lives. These enemies are anxiety, worry, doubt, discouragement, and defeat, to name a few. We are anxious about our financial situation. We worry about our children's choices. We doubt God's care for us. We get discouraged when our efforts seem futile. We get defeated by the opinions of others. These enemies are like terrorists and attack when we least expect it and are least prepared. They undermine our security and self-worth and are far more subtle and damaging than those wearing military garb and carrying guns.

But God is just as real today as he was in Jehoshaphat's day. He is able to deliver. We must follow Jehoshaphat's example and go to God, acknowledging who He is and our dependence on Him, trusting Him to fight for us. The battle is His, not ours. We cannot stand in our own strength or power or figure it out. Our job is to stand back and let God work. He is able to deliver.

Take a moment and name the fears and insecurities that keep you from being steadfast like Jehoshaphat, believing God will deliver you from your enemy. Acknowledge who God is and your dependence on Him. Tell Him what you are facing, and ask Him for deliverance.

God of strength and deliverance,
Too often I fail to trust Your willingness to care for
my life and needs. Forgive me. Today I face_____
and acknowledge Your power and might. I am
dependent on You. Please help me. Thank You.
Amen.

part seven

Rest in His Peace

Day 49

His Peace Is Present

> *Peace I leave with you; My peace I give to you;*
> *not as the world gives, do I give to you.*
> *Let not your heart be troubled, nor let it be fearful.*
> John 14:27

HOW DO YOU DEFINE peace? Lack of conflict, lack of stress, having comforts and wealth? Perhaps peace conjures up thoughts of a vacation from responsibilities. We could expend a great deal of energy working toward such things and still not find the peace we long for. Peace is a gift from Jesus to us, yet so few of us experience it.

Jesus' peace is different from the kind the world gives. His peace does not mean a lack of conflict. You can have His peace in the midst of conflict, in the midst of poverty, in the midst of a stressful situation. Jesus' peace is related to His presence. "Even though

I walk through the valley of the shadow of death, I fear no evil; for Thou art with me" (Psalm 23:4). His presence brought the psalmist peace in a dark and fearful place.

How can we learn to better trust God? We can read His Word and believe what it says—by faith. We cannot go by feelings or even experiences—those can be very subjective. We must take Him at His word and act on it. We may take baby steps at first, but the more we realize we can count on Him and His word, the more secure we will become, and our peace will grow in spite of the circumstances around us. We grow in relationship with Him. He promises us His peace, then tells us, "Let not your heart be troubled, nor let it be fearful." That is a choice. He has given us what we need; now the response is our choice.

Take a moment and remember a time when you felt insecure and fearful. What brought you peace? Was it the presence of someone you loved? God is always with us. He can be trusted never to leave us, to give us His peace. Will you believe that you are secure in His love? He offers you His peace. Will you make the choice to believe Him?

Giver of peace,
I confess that I am fearful and anxious. I don't
know what tomorrow will bring. I want to feel se-
cure with You—please help me. I choose to trust
Your promises. Thank You for giving me Your
peace and always being with me. Amen.

Day 50

His Peace Is Promising

*Yield now and be at peace with Him;
thereby good will come to you.*
Job 22:21

PEACE WITH GOD ALL boils down to a relationship, doesn't it? I like the way the King James Version puts this verse, "acquaint now thyself with Him and be at peace." In the margin of my Bible it says that "yield" can be read as "know intimately." When we know God, intimately, in a day-to-day relationship, we know peace regardless of what circumstances may be assaulting us.

What does it take to know someone intimately? You must spend time with that person, talk with him, listen to him. You may write letters back and forth. You want to learn how he thinks. You want to know what he likes and dislikes. You want to meet his friends. You try to please him and anticipate his needs. An intimate relationship isn't developed quickly—but deeply over time. It is built on trust.

An intimate relationship with God is developed much the same way. We spend time with Him by reading what He has to say, talking to Him about everything—big and small—and listening for His voice. He has revealed Himself in Scripture. There He will let you know how He thinks and what He thinks about you. So the best way to get to know Him is to spend time studying His Word and being around others who are seeking an intimate relationship with Him as well. As you grow in your relationship with God, you will be more eager to do the things that please Him. You will discover that He is true to His word. He is trustworthy. And you will fall deeply in love with Him.

Acquaint yourself with Him—get to know Him intimately—and be at peace. Knowing Him brings peace. Peace will not depend on circumstances but on the relationship you have with the God of peace through His Son, Jesus Christ. And the promise is that "good will come to you." The good is not necessarily our definition of "good"—but His. Peace—a peace that passes understanding, eternal life.

Take a moment and ask yourself in what specific way you can begin to develop a more intimate walk with God. Do you need to confess a sin in your life that is blocking intimacy? Do you need to spend more time in His Word? In prayer? Ask God by His

Holy Spirit to reveal to you His heart and longing for you.

All-knowing and loving Father,
I admit I have a long way to go, but I want to
know You intimately so that the circumstances of
my life cannot disturb the peace I have deep in my
heart. I confess that all too often I let circum-
stances control me. I choose to give them to You
now and ask Your Holy Spirit to take control, giv-
ing me the peace that only You can give. Help me
to develop an intimate relationship with You.
Thank You. Amen.

Day 51

His Peace Is Powerful

> *The* LORD *is Peace.*
> Judges 6:24

THE LORD IS A holy God. Powerful. In the Old
Testament He was beyond human experience.
Humans had no way to relate to Him. When He
showed up, He was disguised or hidden in order to
protect humans. His presence was overwhelming.
It was described in terms of fire, thunder, lightning,
and earthquake. No one could even approach the
Holy of Holies and live.

And yet here we have one of the names of the
Lord as *Peace*. How does one put that together—a
terrifying presence and peace? They do not contradict. The Lord is holy, and the Lord is peace. His holiness gives His peace authority. His power gives His
peace security.

When I was a young girl, I traveled to New York City by train from my home in North Carolina. We would wait for the train to pull into the station. It rumbled into town, the earth shook, the whistle blew, and it hissed to a stop. I found it frightening, but my mother made sure I got on board safely and under the care of the kind porter. The train would begin to roll away from the station. Once safely inside my cabin, watching the scenery glide past my window, I no longer felt the ground shake or heard the loud whistle. I felt safe. I was at peace inside the security of that powerful and terrifying train.

That is how we can experience the Lord. When we live outside of His care, not in a personal relationship with Him, living in our own way and on our own power, life can be terrifying. Frightening. Our ground does shake. The noise around us is incessant and unbearable. How do we discern what to listen to? How do we find stability? Instead of fighting with the Lord, we need to climb aboard. Find peace in the security of who He is. He is peace.

Take a moment. Are you feeling insecure? Lacking peace? Does the Lord seem more frightening than peaceful? Think of the train. Outside, it is intimidating, but once you climb aboard and commit to it, you are safe. You are carried by it. Commit yourself to the Lord's care.

Lord of peace,
I admit that I think of You as frightening. I feel
that I am not good enough to approach You, that
You will be angry with me and punish me rather
than invite and welcome me. I do not have peace.
My world is shaking. Please help me find peace. By
faith, I commit myself to You and ask that You give
me Your peace. Thank You. Amen.

His Peace Guards You

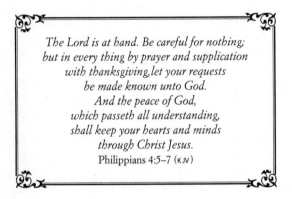

*The Lord is at hand. Be careful for nothing;
but in every thing by prayer and supplication
with thanksgiving, let your requests
be made known unto God.
And the peace of God,
which passeth all understanding,
shall keep your hearts and minds
through Christ Jesus.*
Philippians 4:5–7 (KJV)

I LOVE THIS SCRIPTURE. I memorized it early in life, but I only learned verses 6 and 7. The important key is what comes just before: "The Lord is at hand." It is because He is near that you do not have to be anxious. He is nearby and in control. The almighty God is close at hand, watching over you.

Your job is to talk to Him about everything. Ask

for His help, wisdom, and guidance. Ask for His patience and love. But when you are asking, remember to couple it with gratitude. Thank Him for your redemption. Thank Him for life. He is the One who made you in your mother's womb. Thank Him for what He has done for you in the past. There is so much to thank Him for—so much to talk to Him about.

His promise to you is that His peace will guard your heart and mind. Such peace is of a heavenly nature and so cannot be understood by mere mortals. It is more substantial and lasting than we can possibly understand. So don't try. Just trust. This peace guards both our hearts and our minds—our ability to think and reason and know, as well as our emotions and feelings. All have to be guarded and kept in balance.

This can only he accomplished through Christ Jesus. He is the One who gives this peace that keeps watch over our emotions and reason. And who better to do it than Jesus? He became what we are—fully human—so He can understand what we experience and the temptations we face. We cannot understand it, but we can say, "Thank you."

Take a moment and recognize God's nearness to you at this moment. Begin to make a list of the things for which you are grateful. Talk to Him about everything on your mind and heart. Tell Him everything. Ask Him for what you need. Do you need peace, patience, guidance? Ask Him. And take the peace He promised—the kind that is substantial and lasting. Then thank Him for understanding you and loving you.

Grantor of heavenly peace,
Thank You for being close. I so often forget how
close You really are and that Your peace is ready to
stand guard over my heart and mind. Forgive me
for ignoring Your presence and gifts. I confess that
I do not have a grateful heart—help me to culti-
vate one that is quick to recognize and respond to
Your gifts in my life. I need Your peace and I thank
You for giving it to me. Amen.

Day 53

His Peace Is Perfect

The steadfast of mind Thou wilt keep in perfect peace,
because he trusts in Thee.
Trust in the LORD forever, for in GOD the LORD,
we have an everlasting Rock.
Isaiah 26:3–4

WHO DOESN'T WANT "PERFECT peace"? A peace that is undisturbed, complete, unqualified. But in our uncertain world, where do we find such peace? This scripture says the person with a steadfast mind is the one who will have perfect peace. What does it mean to have a steadfast mind? It means to focus on something and not take your mind off of it. Don't even blink. What do we focus on? God and His character. As we trust and stay steadfast, we will receive perfect peace. Trust + steadfast mind = perfect peace.

I find it very difficult to keep a steadfast mind. There are so many things that take my focus off of God. Just little things like an unexpected interruption that throws my whole day off and makes me fret over whether I can meet that deadline that is looming. Or one of my car's warning lights comes on, and I imagine my car needs major repairs. Immediately my focus goes to "what ifs." Fretting sets in, and before I know it, I have been sucked into a downward spiral and have lost my focus on God. I blinked. The Enemy loves that and uses it to his advantage. That's why I find it helpful to have verses about God's character or praise music playing as reminders around the house and in my car. He is sufficient. He is in control. These tools help me draw my focus back to God as my Rock. He has it all under control.

The object of our trust is the Lord, and we can trust Him forever. He is eternal, and all of His character qualities are eternal. We never need to doubt that His trustworthiness will end or evaporate. He is an everlasting Rock. What could be more secure than that? In Him, the everlasting Rock, we have perfect peace.

Take a moment and think about the things that cause you to blink and tie you in knots, robbing you of peace. Write this verse out on a 3 x 5 card, and put it in a place where you will see it. Maybe you need to make several—one for your bathroom mirror, one for your kitchen window, and one for your car's dash. Do what you need to do to be reminded of His care for you. He is your eternal Rock.

Eternal Rock,
I want perfect peace. I want to stay focused on You.
But I confess that I easily blink and lose focus. I
focus on the small irritations and interruptions
rather than Your eternal character qualities. Help
me to refocus on You. Thank You for being my
secure eternal Rock and for being the giver of
perfect peace. Amen.

Day 54

His Peace Is Certain

> *Cease striving and know that I am God;*
> *I will be exalted among the nations,*
> *I will be exalted in the earth.*
> *The LORD of hosts is with us.*
> Psalm 46:10–11

STRIVING. THE WORD ACTUALLY makes me tired. I imagine a man lifting a heavy load, his muscles bulging, his veins popping out on his arms, sweat beading on his forehead. Striving. Work. Effort. This scripture says "Stop!" Cease. Let go. Relax. Pause. Quit. Your efforts will not get you where you want. Let God be God.

Why is it so hard to quit, let go, relax? Because we want to be in control. We associate control with security and comfort, and we don't want to let go. We live in an uncertain world and nothing seems secure, so we grab for any control we can hang on to. But that is not God's way, and any control we do have is just an illusion.

This verse tells us that God will be exalted among the nations and in the earth. As we watch our world's political systems stagger toward self-destruction, it is good to stop and focus on the fact that God will be exalted. He is on His throne, and it cannot be shaken.

That is security. We can relax. As we hear reports of our earth's resources being used up and abused, it is comforting to know He will be exalted in the earth. This global sphere on which we live belongs to Him. The earth is His creation. He watches over it and keeps it. That is comforting.

This verse tells us that "the LORD of hosts is with us." In all of the uncertainties and insecurities, in our attempts to gain and maintain control, He is with us. He has it under control, and we need to be still. As long as we are worrying over what we cannot control, we get in God's way and fail to see that He "will be exalted among the nations." Get quiet and know Him. Our highest priority is to know Him, to worship Him. But we cannot do that when we are still grasping for control—the two are mutually exclusive.

Take a moment and get still. Breathe deeply, then let it out slowly. What are you trying to control? The outcome of your day? Your spouse's decisions? Your children's friendships? How people perceive you? Do you really have any control over any of it? Think of

God being with you right this minute. Open your hands and relinquish control to Him. Now praise Him for His control and that He has good plans for your life.

God Almighty,
I confess that I do try to control the things in my life. I want them to run smoothly so that I will feel secure and comfortable. But I am tired and stressed. I quit. I give it to You. I want You to help me be still and know You. Thank You. Amen.

His Peace Is Comforting

> *Thou art my hiding place;*
> *Thou dost preserve me from trouble;*
> *Thou dost surround me with songs of deliverance.*
> Psalm 32:7

DO YOU JUST EVER want to run away and hide? Have you ever said, "Stop the world, I want to get off"? Pressures got to you? The final straw did you in, and you have had enough? The psalmist said it well, "Oh, that I had wings like a dove! I would fly away and be at rest. . . . I would hasten to my place of refuge from the stormy wind and tempest" (Psalm 55:6, 8). Have you felt that way? You need a break. You need a place of refuge, a place of comfort and security. And you need it now. But Tahiti is out of the question! Besides, you are in the middle of life, have decisions to make, people counting on you, projects due, and schedules to keep. There is no break in sight.

David knew where to go. It wasn't Tahiti or any exotic destination. He went to the Lord, his hiding place. Scripture says God is a refuge, a rock, a fortress—all that indicates a safe place to find security and comfort.

David knew God would preserve him from trouble. How? Was David seeking a life of ease without problems? An escape? I think not. I believe David was still in the midst of the struggle. God wasn't going to remove David's tribulation and enemies—that is not usually God's plan. He wants us to grow strong in the struggle. He will sustain us in the midst of life. Life comes fraught with trouble, and God wants us to run to Him to find comfort, strength, help, wisdom, guidance. God has us in His secure love, and He promises to care for us in the pressures of life.

Not only will He care for us, but He will give us songs of deliverance and *surround* us with songs of deliverance. Not weapons for deliverance. Not a plan for deliverance. But songs. Praise is a powerful tool to defeat the Enemy. It gets our focus back on God and off the problems that seem so overwhelming. It lifts our hearts. That's why I like to have praise music playing on my office stereo all day long.

Yes, He is our secure hiding place. He preserves us from trouble by sustaining us through the power of the Holy Spirit. He preserves us in the pressures and stress of life. And He gives us songs to help us get our focus back on Him.

Take a moment and think of a time when you could not get a song out of your head. You kept humming it over and over, and it became the backdrop of the day or experience. That is what God wants to be for us. A song in our day, in our hearts, in our lives. Sing the Doxology, and allow it to lift your focus to Him. Let this be your song of praise today. Thank Him for all that He is for you today and every day—your hiding place and sustainer.

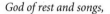

God of rest and songs,
I am feeling overwhelmed by life, and I have taken
my eyes off of You. Forgive me. I want You to be
my hiding place, my shelter in the storm. Please
give me the sustaining strength and wisdom I need
as well as songs of deliverance. Thank You. Amen.

His Peace Is Inviting

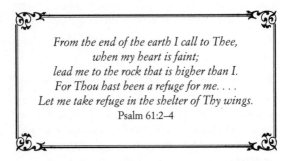

From the end of the earth I call to Thee,
when my heart is faint;
lead me to the rock that is higher than I.
For Thou hast been a refuge for me. . . .
Let me take refuge in the shelter of Thy wings.
Psalm 61:2–4

As a frequent traveler, I have felt like I have been to the end of the earth and back. As my sister Anne once said, when we were traveling under less-than-ideal circumstances and far from home and security, "We are not at the end of the earth, but we can see it from here." No matter where we are, we can call on God. His ear is always tuned in to our cry.

Near my home, off the Blue Ridge Parkway, is an area of rocks called Humpback Rock. When you climb up there, you can see across the Shenandoah

Valley to the Alleghany Mountains beyond. It is a high rock and allows those who climb it to see above and beyond. There are times we need such a place, to be able to see above our needs and beyond our problems. God is that place. He is "the rock that is higher than I." He invites me to come to Him to get His perspective.

I know I have been at the end of my rope! And losing my grip fast. Life has a way of becoming overwhelming quickly. I have felt overwhelmed by life. My heart was broken. People's opinions came uninvited. I needed to make decisions. I was concerned for my children. I was not able to rest. My health was suffering. Peace was elusive. I remember driving to my parents' home and seeing the mountains in the distance. Finally driving through the gates and walking through the door, I knew I was safe. God is a refuge that does not depend on place or time. He is always there.

I love that phrase "the shelter of Thy wings." Doesn't it sound inviting and cozy? It sounds like a place of renewal and refreshment, like wrapping yourself in a down blanket! We can rest there. His wings cover and protect us, shelter and hide us. God provides that for us and welcomes us when we come.

Take a moment to think about the stresses of your life. Is life closing in on you? Are problems overwhelming you? Do you need a new perspective? Call out to the rock that is higher than you are. He is listening and waiting. He is your refuge and shelter. He invites you in and welcomes you with open arms.

Sheltering God,
I have been going around in circles, trying to do
things in my own strength. Life is closing in fast. I
am worn out—at the end of my rope. I need
You—the Rock that is higher than I. I need to see
above the things that stress me out. I need Your
perspective. I need Your shelter and peace. Thank
You for being there for me at all times and in any
place. Please help me. Thank You. Amen.

part eight

Hear His Invitation

He Invites You
to Quench Your Thirst

> *Ho! Every one who thirsts, come to the waters;*
> *and you who have no money come, buy and eat.*
> *Come, buy wine and milk without money*
> *and without cost.*
> *Why do you spend money for what is not bread,*
> *and your wages for what does not satisfy?*
> *Listen carefully to Me, and eat what is good,*
> *and delight yourself in abundance.*
>
> Isaiah 55:1–2

ARE YOU THIRSTY? FOR WHAT? What do you long for? What are you pursuing? What do you spend your time dreaming about? This passage calls us to examine ourselves. What are we doing? Are we pursuing the things that do not satisfy? So often we wear ourselves out trying to be more, do more, have more. And yet it does not fulfill us—there is always more out there beckoning us. One more hill to climb. One more achievement.

This verse tells us to *stop!* Instead of the relentless pursuit of things that do not satisfy, He invites everyone to come. Come to Him, the *living water*. It isn't an exclusive offer for those who have it all together—it is for everyone. Drug addicts pursuing the next high. Prostitutes seeking the next trick. Bankers after the next deal. Preachers trying to look good. Sinners pursing that which does not satisfy. We are all sinners. The invitation is for all. Come to the water. Be cleansed. Refreshed. Imagine a cool, clear watering hole where children are playing—diving, splashing, playing. Carefree. We all long to be free from the burdens and sins we carry. Such freedom is possible.

What He offers is free. Money is not the currency of His kingdom; faith and trust are. What we receive from Him is always the best. He says, "I would feed you with the finest of the wheat; and with honey from the rock I would satisfy you" (Psalm 81:16). He longs to satisfy us. He wants us to delight in His abundance of peace, grace, forgiveness, mercy, love, and joy. It can't be bought. It can only be received.

God is not stingy. He pours good things out upon us if we would but stop running after that which is empty. Stop grasping at things you will ultimately lose, and open your hand to receive eternal, lasting gifts. You will be glad you did.

Take a moment. What occupies your thoughts and energy? Does it have eternal value? Stop running after that which has no lasting value. For what is your heart longing? Have you found it? You have a standing invitation to come to the living water that cleanses, refreshes, and satisfies in abundance.

Living Water,
I confess that I am wearing myself out in the pursuit of an elusive satisfaction. I want to stop but don't know how. I do not pursue You with my whole heart and I grow weary in my half-hearted attempts to know You. You freely offer that which satisfies, no striving, no grasping, no struggling. Forgive me for not delighting in and thanking You for your abundant gifts to me. Help me to open my heart and life to You. Thank You. Amen.

He Invites You
to Renew Your Mind

*Do not be conformed to this world,
but be transformed by the renewing of your mind,
that you may prove what the will of God is,
that which is good and acceptable and perfect.*
Romans 12:2

W E LIVE IN A world of conformity. Peer pressure is a powerful agent for conformity. We all fall into its pervasive trap. This passage tells us not to be conformed to the standards and pursuits of this world. But how do we do this? By being transformed—changed from the inside out.

I don't know about you, but when I set out to transform myself—be it exercise, diet, or any self-help program—I am not very good at it. I don't stick to it for very long. I get sidetracked, discouraged, or just fall back into old habits that are more comfortable. This passage tells us that we can change, be transformed, by the renewing of our minds. The mind is powerful. We all have tapes that play in our heads. Self-talk can be very powerful, either for negative or positive input and reinforcement. The choice is ours.

This passage says that to renew our minds is to come to understand God's will for our lives which is good, acceptable, and perfect. I like how The Message puts it, "Unlike the culture around you, always dragging you down to its level of immaturity, God brings the best out of you, develops well-formed maturity in you." That's what I want for my life.

Renewing our minds is first a decision, then a process. Once we make the decision to renew our minds, the Holy Spirit will come alongside and inhabit that decision and help us do it. I find it helpful to find a verse that speaks to the issue troubling me. I write it out and post it in places where I will see it regularly. I begin to memorize it. And when my mind begins to fret about whatever issue it may be, I read that verse and let its truth sink into my mind and heart.

Begin with just a sentence like, "God is able." Replay that in your mind when things look impossible, when you are frustrated or hurting. It is simple, yet it isn't always easy. Remember, we can call on the help of the Holy Spirit who eagerly desires for us to be transformed. Begin today.

Take a moment and choose to renew your mind

about whatever is weighing you down. Find a Bible verse that speaks to that issue. Read the verse slowly and thoughtfully. Roll it over in your mind. Write it out. Let the truth of it sink in. Now post it where you will see it frequently. You are on the way to transforming your mind!

Transforming God,
I confess that I am easily swayed and conformed
by the world's standards. I want to be conformed
to You and Your will. Transform me and help me
to renew my mind by the power of the Holy Spirit.
Thank You. Amen.

He Invites You to Be Satisfied

*I satisfy the weary ones
and refresh everyone who languishes.*
Jeremiah 31:25

GOD IS SPEAKING HERE. He is the One who satisfies the weary ones. Are you weary today? Weary of routine? Has life lost some of its meaning and joy as if all seems to be in the color gray? Are you just putting one foot in front of the other? Perhaps you have begun to wonder what the purpose of your life is. You have a longing in your soul that nothing seems to fill, as if you are hungry for something but you aren't quite sure what it is. But it gnaws at you constantly, bringing with it a dull sense of dissatisfaction.

That is not God's desire or plan for you. He doesn't just want you to endure; He wants you to flourish. He wants to satisfy the weary one. "For He has satisfied the thirsty soul, and the hungry soul He has filled with what is good" (Psalm 107:9). God doesn't fill us with fluff—He brings substantial supplies that give life meaning and purpose. His joy. His strength. His hope. His peace. His love. He who put the colors in the rainbow can put the color back into your life. He longs to do that for you.

He says He refreshes everyone who languishes—those who have grown weak and fallen to the back. He doesn't condemn or chastise. He knows what has made you tired and unable to keep up. He knows the battles you have fought. He knows the wounds you have sustained. He knows how you have tried to persevere but now have grown weak in the struggle.

I picture a weary soldier beside the road, wounded, tired, no longer able to keep up with his comrades. About to give up. But God Himself looks on with compassion and love. Gently He picks up the languishing one and carries him to a place of refreshing. What would refresh one who has grown weak and fallen back? The one languishing doesn't need a pep talk or to be told what to do to get back up. No. He needs gentleness, comfort, care, and nourishment. He needs time to regain his strength and perspective. He needs encouragement. God "gives strength to the weary, and to him who lacks might He increases power. . . . Those who wait for the LORD will gain new strength. . . . They will walk and not become weary" (Isaiah 40:29, 31). The key is to wait on the Lord. Quit trying in your own strength. Wait, and He will give you His.

Take a moment and write down the things that have made you weary and grow weak. Is it a defeat? Is it unending stress? Maybe it isn't anything dramatic. Maybe it is the day-to-day routine of your life. Talk to God about it—tell Him. He understands and seeks to give His strength, His joy, His peace. Ask for it and settle for no less. Be willing to wait on Him— He comes at the right time with His gifts.

God of the weary,
I confess that I have grown weary in the battle. I
am ready to quit. I need Your refreshing, Your
supply that satisfies completely. But I need the
patience to wait for Your timing. Please help me.
Thank You. Amen.

He Invites You to Be Refreshed

> *Repent therefore and return,*
> *that your sins may be wiped away,*
> *in order that times of refreshing*
> *may come from the presence of the Lord.*
> Acts 3:19

AFTER WORKING IN MY yard all of a hot summer day, I am tired, my clothes are sticking to my body, I am covered with perspiration and dirt. I step into my shower and let the cool water rinse away the grime and sweat. It also soothes my aching muscles, and I step out clean and invigorated. It feels so good to be clean and fresh.

That in a small way illustrates what Peter is talking about in this passage when he speaks of repentance and being refreshed. Repentance means to agree with God that we are covered with the sweat and grime of sin—trying to live life our way and failing at it. We make the decision to turn from our sin and ask Jesus to take over. He washes away our sin, and refreshing comes to our spirit.

I don't know the sin with which you struggle most—anxiety, fear, anger, lack of gratitude, pride. You know what it is. You have tried your best to overcome it and keep sliding back into the same sin—over and over again. You are sick of it. God doesn't want you to live that way. You don't have to. You can be free. Confess to Him your sin, and ask Him to forgive you. God forgives freely and completely. You can be restored and refreshed to start anew.

The refreshment He gives is eternal—from the very realms of heaven. It comes from the actual presence of the Lord. He will refresh you with Himself. When we repent, He brings all of His resources to us to revive and restore us—peace, joy, gentleness, love, patience, kindness, goodness, self-control, faithfulness (see Galatians 5:22–23). These are the fruit of His Spirit living in us as we yield to His presence in us. We are then free and enabled to live and serve Him.

Take a moment and close your eyes. What brings you a sense of refreshment? A cool shower on a hot day? A walk along the beach? Listening to your favorite music? Being with friends? Put yourself there and enjoy it. Now think about what is going on in your inner core. Are you experiencing anxiety, turmoil, fear? Talk to God about it.

Source of all refreshment,
I confess to You that I live in a constant state of
turmoil. I am sick of living life that way. That is
sin. I am sorry, and I ask You to help me change. I
come to You to be refreshed. Please wash away my
sin and fill me with Your Spirit. Refresh me to
serve You and live in Your peace. Thank You.
Amen.

He Invites You to Trust

> *I know whom I have believed*
> *and am persuaded that he is able to keep that*
> *which I have committed unto him against that day.*
> 2 Timothy 1:12 (KJV)

WHEN WE GIVE SOMEONE something of value to keep for us until we need it, we place trust in that person. I put money in the bank and trust it to keep it safe until I need to write a check. When I tell my friend something important, I trust her to keep it confidential. But before we trust someone, we need to know if she is trustworthy. No doubt we have all felt the sting of placing our trust in someone who let us down. It made us wary to trust again. We felt insecure and betrayed.

How do we learn if someone or something is trustworthy? At first we test the waters. We talk to her, get to know her. We observe how she handles other people; we may ask about her reputation and integrity. Then we begin to trust her with little things, and if she proves to be true, we move to trust her a bit more until, in time, we are confiding the deep things of our heart to her.

We can do this with God too. We get to know Him through His Word and prayer. We ask others about their experience with how He has been faithful to them. We observe His work in the lives of others. And when we are ready, we begin to trust Him with little things in life. Then with big things.

The above verse is one I have written out and placed on my car dashboard. It is there to remind me that God is able to keep that which I give to Him. I have given Him my heart. I have given Him my soul to keep. I have given Him my marriage, my children, and my grandchildren—He is able to keep them. I have given Him my house, finances, friendships, and future. He has it all, and He is able to handle it all for safekeeping. I have found Him to be trustworthy throughout my life.

Take a moment and think about your most trusted confidant and all she knows about you. Have you opened your heart to God like you have opened it to her? God wants to hear your innermost thoughts because He desires an intimate relationship with you.

Trustworthy God,
Thank You for being able to keep the big and small
things in my life. I confess that my trust is weak
and feeble. Help me to grow in trust. Thank You
for caring about me and inviting me to draw closer
to You each day. Help me to remove the barriers
that keep me from completely trusting You. Thank
You. Amen.

Day 62

He Invites You to Find Strength

> *As thy days, so shall thy strength be.*
> Deuteronomy 33:25 (KJV)

MY MOTHER GAVE ME a little card with this verse printed on it years ago when I went away to boarding school. I have carried it in my Bible and in my purse; now it is under the blotter on my desk. It is stained, and the edges show wear, but it is very dear to me. I look at it every day as I face the tasks ahead to be reminded that God will give me the strength I need for each day. He doesn't give me tomorrow's strength today. He gives me what I need just for today.

God invites us to trust Him for the strength we need each day. "Those who wait for the LORD will gain new strength; they will mount up with wings like eagles, they will run and not get tired, they will walk and not become weary" (Isaiah 40:31). How

wonderful is that! It is His promise to us as we wait
on Him.

Waiting on Him rather than getting impatient
or running out ahead can be hard. Waiting is a discipline. If I see a task at hand, I like to get started
and get it done. I like to check things off my to-do
list. And I have a tendency to overbook myself. For
some reason when I see an empty spot on my calendar, I think it needs to be filled! But then I look
ahead and wonder how it will all get done. I get
filled with anxiety and become stressed. That is not
God's desire for me. I must remind myself, "As thy
days, so shall thy strength be." If God has called me
to these tasks, then I must step into each task, believing He will provide the strength and energy required to carry them out.

Perhaps a busy schedule is not your challenge.
You may be facing surgery or waiting for the results
of medical tests, and you don't think you have the
strength to face it. Perhaps you are struggling with
an addiction and are not sure you have what it takes
to break it. Or a loved one has died, and you don't
think you can cope alone. God promises, "As thy
days, so shall thy strength be." He gives you what you
need when you need it. He invites you to gain your
strength from Him. You do not have to do it in your
own strength, and you are not alone; He is right
there with you.

Take a moment and think about what lies ahead
for you. Then remember a time when you felt overwhelmed and God met you in a special way. He gave

you His strength and got you through it. Begin to thank Him for the way He provided, and then praise Him that He will give you the strength you need now.

Strong God,
I feel so weak as I face_____. I don't have what it takes, but You do. I feel overwhelmed by fear and anxiety. That is not what You want for me. Build my trust that You'll keep Your promise to give me the strength to meet each day as it comes. Thank You for Your strength that meets my weakness. Amen.

He Invites You
to Receive His Blessing

> *Blessed be the God*
> *and Father of our Lord Jesus Christ,*
> *who has blessed us with every spiritual blessing*
> *in the heavenly places in Christ.*
> Ephesians 1:3

I CANNOT BEGIN TO IMAGINE what "every spiritual blessing in the heavenly places in Christ" encompasses. In the Bible a blessing is a gift from God with no strings attached. God is the gift giver. His supply is endless. He never runs out, never shortchanges us. He gives us every spiritual good thing: forgiveness, redemption, restoration, peace, joy, grace, holiness, acceptance, wisdom, comfort, power, rest, sustenance, victory, justice, protection, strength, mercy, understanding, holiness. The list could go on. Have fun adding to this list—*every* spiritual blessing.

"In the heavenly places" means they are the best, the finest, the highest. Superlative. What amazes me is that these are God's gifts to me—He blesses me with these things because He loves me. I am His child, and like a loving father, He gives His children what they need to live obedient, fulfilled, and fruitful lives. He invites us to partake of these blessings in Christ Jesus. They are not ours apart from Him.

How does knowing that the Creator of the universe gives you gifts affect the way you live your life?

We are not to hoard our blessings and keep them to ourselves. We are to pass them on. That is what a heavenly blessing is for—to be used in service to others—to be given away. You have been given forgiveness—now pass on forgiveness to someone who has wounded you. You have been given joy—now pass on some joy to those in your home. You have been given comfort. Now pass on that comfort to another. God's followers are the original "re-gifters."

Take a moment to write down some of the gifts that you have been given, and thank God for them. Now ask yourself if there are ways to more effectively pass on those blessings to others. In your family. Your workplace. Your community. Your church. Make a plan to pass on a blessing you have received to someone else today.

Gracious and giving God,
Thank You for the many blessings You have be-
stowed upon me. I confess that too often I take
them for granted and only think of the things I
want and need in my life. I fail to recognize or ap-
preciate what I have already been given. Forgive
me. Help me to have a grateful heart and turn my
blessings around to bless others. Amen.

Day 64

He Invites You
to Enjoy His Company

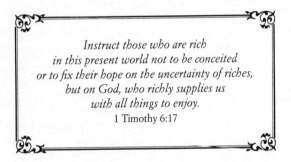

*Instruct those who are rich
in this present world not to be conceited
or to fix their hope on the uncertainty of riches,
but on God, who richly supplies us
with all things to enjoy.*
1 Timothy 6:17

So often, sadly, we do not associate the word *enjoy* with God. We think of Him as austere, harsh, unapproachable. We fear that He is up in heaven just waiting for us to mess up so He can "get us." Many of us think of God as we think of a parent when we have done something wrong. We think, *I know I am going to get it now.* Nothing could be further from the truth. God has given us life to enjoy.

The world tells us that enjoyment can be

bought. We acquire a lot of stuff to insulate us from the harshness of the world. But it is the world that is harsh—not God. It is Satan that has turned our thoughts around to make us think wrongly. He makes the world look enjoyable and God look fierce. Stuff wears out, breaks, loses its luster, and has to be paid for. True joy comes from God—the way a baby snuggles up against your neck, the laughter of a child, the beauty of an eagle soaring in the air, the sunset over the ocean. These cannot be bought. They are gifts for us from our loving heavenly Father.

God does not say that the things the world provides are wrong or bad, but He instructs us to keep them in perspective. He invites us to enjoy everything—it is all a gift from Him. Jesus told us in John 10:10 that "The thief comes only to steal and kill and destroy; I came that they have life, and might have it abundantly." God invites us to enjoy life.

I had a great pioneer missionary friend, Jerry Rose, who is now in heaven. He pioneered the Balim Valley in Irian Jaya, Indonesia. He would fascinate us by the hour with stories of his adventures, the sights he saw, the native peoples he encountered, the miracles he witnessed. I recall his telling us of trekking into the jungle and coming upon a little pool of water. He stopped to rest for a bit, and as he looked into the pool, he saw very delicate, bright blue flowers growing in the water. As far as he knew, no other human had ever been where he was, and it occurred to him that God had placed that beauty there for him to see and for his enjoyment. "*God . . . supplies us with all things to enjoy.*"

Take a moment to think about what brings you true joy. Make a list and begin to thank God for those things in your life. Begin to enjoy them more fully.

Heavenly Father,
Thank You that You have given us all things to
enjoy. I confess that all too often I fail to enjoy the
simple pleasures You bestow on my life. Forgive
me. Today, I want to rejoice in Your abundant life
poured out over me. Thank You. Amen.

part nine

Embrace His Forgiveness

His Forgiveness Is Compassionate

> *The LORD is like a father to his children,*
> *tender and compassionate to those who fear him.*
> *For he knows how weak we are;*
> *he remembers we are only dust.*
> Psalm 103:13–14 (NLT)

Do you often repeat the same mistakes? You just can't seem to learn, so you get frustrated and angry with yourself. Your self-talk is all negative, and soon you find yourself in a pit. You begin to think God sees you as a waste of time—why should He bother with you?

The great King David found himself in a pit of despair (see Psalm 40:2). When David was in such a place, he turned to God and cried for help. He recognized his need and didn't waste time trying to come up with a strategy or plan of his own to get out. God did not chastise him or become angry or impatient with David for being in the pit. He knew David inside and out just as He knows you. God had compassion on David, as He does on you. When God feels compassion, it moves Him to action. God lifted David out of the pit. How? Scripture doesn't tell us exactly, but I would venture to say that God helped David change his focus—to take his eyes off the pit and look to his faithful God.

In Psalm 103 David writes that God is like a father to His children. A perfect father. The kind of father you always longed for. He is available. He listens. He is tender. He is compassionate. He wants us to come to Him with every and any problem. As Creator, God's compassion and concern extends to all, but there is a special connection to those who have chosen to be His children by putting their faith in Jesus.

God understands us. He knows how weak and frail we are; after all, He knows we are made of dust. He Himself made us. He doesn't say to you, *You stupid little piece of dust, why did you do it that way*. He says to us, *You precious little piece of dust; of course you could not have done any better without me.*

He loves you. You are free to come to Him time after time for the same thing. Ask Him to help you overcome by the power of His Holy Spirit. You will receive a warm welcome. He will not turn you away. He will answer with tenderness and compassion.

Take a moment and think about God's compassion—His tenderness and gentleness. Compare that with how you may be feeling about yourself. Tell God about the despair you feel, the pit you are in, and ask Him to help you focus on His compassion instead.

Compassionate Father,
I'm here again. I can't seem to crawl out of this pit.
I feel like dirt. All I can see is the painful cycle I
repeat. I am not sure You want to bother with me,
but You are my last hope. Please help me break the
cycle of repeated sin and despair. I thank You that
You are tender and compassionate. Help me to
focus on that. I need You. Help me. Thank You.
Amen.

His Forgiveness Is Constant

> *God will do this,*
> *for he is faithful to do what he says,*
> *and he has invited you*
> *into partnership with his Son,*
> *Jesus Christ our Lord.*
> 1 Corinthians 1:9 (NLT)

FAITHFULNESS IS A WONDERFUL trait. To be able to be counted on. To be trustworthy. We value faithfulness in such ordinary things as a clock, a car, a computer. We depend on them to function as they were designed to function. It throws a kink into my day when my clock malfunctions or my car fails to start or my computer crashes. In the same way, all of us want faithful people in our lives—a spouse, friends, coworkers. We depend on people to be faithful. But too many of us know the pain of betrayal. The disappointment, disillusionment, and second-guessing that come with unfaithfulness. It is easy to let those wounds make you cynical and bitter, but we are all flawed and all disappoint. No one is perfectly faithful.

Only God. He is faithful all the time, in any situation, under any circumstance. He alone is truly faithful. Others may disappoint us—not God. There are many references to the faithfulness of God in the Bible. It is one of His character traits. He is called "the faithful one" (Isaiah 49:7 NLT). He will do what He says He will do—He is true to His word. But we must know what He has said by studying the Bible, His Word. God's Word is alive and relevant and applicable to our everyday lives.

The Bible tells us that He is faithful to forgive us our sins when we confess them (see 1 John 1:9); He will strengthen and guard us from Satan (see 2 Thessalonians 3:3). He is faithful to keep His covenant (see Deuteronomy 7:9). And part of His covenant with us is to place us in partnership with Jesus. In His holiness He cannot lie (see Psalm 89:35). God's Word is true.

There were times when I was disappointed with God. I felt He had not been true to His word. But I came to realize that I was expecting Him to fulfill His word according to my expectations. I came to see that God wasn't at fault; I was. I needed to let God be God and quit trying to manipulate the Scriptures to fit my need of the moment. I had lost sight of the bigger picture, but all along God knew what He was doing, and He fulfilled His promises to me in ways I could never have imagined. I learned that He is exceedingly faithful to His Word and to me, His child.

　　Take a moment to think about how important faithfulness is to you. Right now thank God that He is faithful. Faithful to His Word and promises. Faithful to you and to those you love. Praise Him that you can depend on Him always and in every situation.

Faithful God,
Thank You so much for being true to Your Word.
That I can count on You to do what You say.
Thank You for forgiving me. Thank You for pro-
tecting and guarding me from evil. Thank You for
the abundant blessings You so faithfully pour out
in my life—life itself, rest in sleep, food, shelter,
family, and friends. You are faithful to me. Open
my eyes that I might see even more of Your faith-
fulness. Thank You. Amen.

His Forgiveness Is Renewing

If any man is in Christ, he is a new creature;
the old things passed away;
behold, new things have come.
2 Corinthians 5:17

WOULD YOU LIKE TO begin again? Start over? You can. The Bible talks a lot about new things. It says that when we give our lives to Christ, we become new persons. We start new lives. We can put the past behind us. One of Satan's tactics is to make us doubt this fact. He would convince us that we are condemned to continue to live in the old way, that we are stuck and cannot change. Jesus died to set us free from our sins and our pasts. However, that does not mean we are perfect.

Then what is this new life? What is this talking about? Nicodemus was confused, too, so he asked

Jesus what it was all about. Jesus told him that it wasn't physical life but spiritual life (see John 3:1–21). Our new life is a spiritual life. He has put His Spirit in us, which begins the process of transforming us. We still have the same personalities and temperaments, but as we yield to His Spirit, our new spiritual lives grow stronger.

He promises "I will give you a new heart and put a new spirit within you; and I will remove the heart of stone from your flesh and give you a heart of flesh. And I will put My Spirit within you and cause you to walk in My statutes, and you will be careful to observe My ordinances" (Ezekiel 36:26–27). He works in us by His Spirit; we don't have to do this spiritual work on our own. We do, however, have to cooperate and embrace it, and He will enable us. He does a new thing in us (see Jeremiah 31:22).

God gives us gifts for this new life. He not only gives us new hearts and spirits, He gives us a new song, new joy, new peace. He gives us new names. Names are important in Scripture—they indicate character. We are each given a new character—His. He says He will give us new purpose to our lives. Lasting purpose.

Yes, the old is behind us; the new has begun. Embrace it.

Take a moment and think about newness. What do you want to become new in your life? Your heart? Your spirit? A relationship? A purpose? A habit? Tell God. Look up the Scriptures in this devotional and claim all that He has given you.

God of new beginnings,
Thank You for the new life You have given me in
Jesus. I confess that I don't understand it all, but I
want to cooperate with Your Spirit in me. I want
the newness You give. I embrace it. Thank You.
Amen.

His Forgiveness Is Secure

> "The mountains may be removed
> and the hills may shake, but
> My lovingkindness will not be removed from you,
> and My covenant of peace will not be shaken,"
> says the LORD who has compassion on you.
> Isaiah 54:10

I LIVE IN THE FOOTHILLS of the Blue Ridge Mountains. I love to look out my window and see them in the distance. They make me feel secure. The likelihood of mountains shaking and hills being removed is extremely remote. God is saying that it is more likely that the mountains will shake and the hills will be removed before His lovingkindness to us wears out and His covenant of peace is voided. We are totally secure in His love, His kindness, His peace.

Kindness is manifest in a sympathetic nature.

When we come to God in need of forgiveness, we feel unworthy—sometimes that holds us back from going to Him for forgiveness. Why should a holy God forgive me for the sins I commit and repeat over and over? Doesn't He tire of me? No. He is of a sympathetic nature. He knows our weaknesses and frailties but He does not excuse them or overlook them. Isn't that what the cross of Calvary illustrates so powerfully? His sympathetic nature was so great toward us that He died in our place. We need not fear such a kind God. He has placed His Spirit within us to help us overcome our weakness as we obey Him.

When my three children were young, they would disobey. Did I tire of their saying they were sorry? Never! I loved to have them recognize what they had done wrong and that they could come to me, knowing I would forgive, love, and help them. It would have broken my heart if I knew they were afraid of me and cowered in my presence, thinking I would turn them away. They knew I wouldn't beat them, belittle them, or reject them. They were secure in my love and kindness toward them.

God is a loving, kind father who wants us to embrace His kindness and focus on His kindness, not our badness. He does not want us to see Him as harsh, hard to please, tyrannical. His Word says over and over that He is kind and loving. "Thou art a God of forgiveness, gracious and compassionate, slow to anger, and abounding in loving kindness" (Nehemiah 9:17). "His lovingkindness is great toward us" (Psalm 117:2).

Take a moment and remember when someone was very kind to you. How did it make you feel? Were you surprised? Did you feel warmed by the kindness? Now think about kindness as one of God's character traits. You need not fear Him. He is sympathetic.

Kind heavenly Father,
How grateful I am that Your lovingkindnesses
never cease and your compassions never fail; they
are new every morning; great is Thy faithfulness.
Amen.

His Forgiveness Is Loving

*We have come to know
and have believed the love which God has for us.
God is love, and the one who abides in love
abides in God, and God abides in him.*
1 John 4:16

GOD MADE US FOR love. God invites us to get to know and embrace His love. What is He offering? Unconditional love. Sacrificial love. That is hard for us to comprehend because we are so accustomed to conditional, selfish relationships—if you do this, then I will love you; if you don't do it, I won't love you. God loved us from the beginning of time just because we are. He gave us the freedom to sin and we did, but He loved us anyway. So wonderful is His love "For one will hardly die for a righteous man; though perhaps for the good man someone would dare even to die. But God demonstrates His own love toward us, in that while we were yet sinners, Christ died for us" (Romans 5:7–8). That is amazing love! We are flawed sinners worthy only of judgment. Yet He loves us. He loves us so much that He sent His only, perfect Son to pay our penalty.

It's hard to believe anyone would love us that much. But He invites us to put our faith in His love and embrace it for our own. God is love. Love originates with Him. It is one of His attributes. Believe it.

How do we abide in love? It is not something we do naturally or manufacture within ourselves. On our own we cannot do it; it is impossible. Love isn't based on feelings. It is based on fact. We embrace the fact of His love. He died for us to demonstrate it. "Whoever confesses that Jesus is the Son of God, God abides in him, and he in God" (1 John 4:15). We must grow to make decisions based on the knowledge of His love though we don't always feel it. Our human nature is to make decisions based on feelings, so consequently our understanding of love ebbs and flows. But God has given us a covenant in His blood, sealed by the Holy Spirit. We embrace it. His Spirit comes to dwell within us and abides there. "By this we know that we abide in Him and He in us, because He has given us of His Spirit" (1 John 4:13).

The evidence of abiding in His love is that we love others. "If we love one another, God abides in us, and His love is perfected in us" (v. 12). It is His love that will flow through us to those around us.

Even the unlovely and difficult. "The one who loves God should love his brother also" (v. 21).

Take a moment and write down the name of someone who needs the touch of God's love today through you. Ask God, by His Spirit, to enable you and give you the opportunity to be His channel of love to that person.

God of love,
Thank you for the love You poured out on me in sending Jesus to die for my sins. Too often I forget and harbor hard feelings toward others. Forgive me. I want Your Spirit to abide in me and enable me to love others for Your sake. Thank You. Amen.

Day 70

His Forgiveness Restores Joy

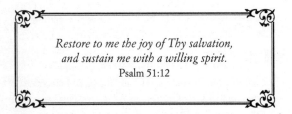

*Restore to me the joy of Thy salvation,
and sustain me with a willing spirit.*
Psalm 51:12

HAVE YOU EVER NOTICED that when you are afraid or anxious, the first thing to go is joy? Fear and anxiety are joy killers. You cannot find joy in the things that used to bring you joy, even simple pleasures. It's as if joy evaporates and gray fog sets in. You manage to do the day-to-day things, but there is no joy, no delight in them.

Depression can rob you of joy quickly. It is a physical condition that can be treated by doctors and counselors. I encourage you, if you think you suffer from depression, to be evaluated by a doctor who understands depression and can help you. Be sure to get rest and exercise and eat healthily—the sun will come out again.

Our enemy, Satan, seeks any way he can to take away our joy. By accusation. People's hurtful comments and opinions. Too busy a schedule. Taking on too many responsibilities. Making sure we are too busy to spend quiet time with God. And, of course, luring us into sin.

Sin kills joy. That is where David was when he wrote this psalm. The prophet Nathan had confronted him about his sin with Bathsheba—the arrogance, disobedience, adultery, lies, murder, and cover-up. David recognized his grave sins against God, confessed them, and asked God to not only cleanse him from his sin, but to restore to him the joy of His salvation and give him a teachable, obedient spirit.

We are sinners. We make a mess of things. But God's specialty is restoration. He loves to take what others might reject as worthless, no good, or damaged and make it useful, restored. He is comfortable with broken people. He sees our potential. He gives us a chance to begin again by giving us teachable and obedient hearts.

Take a moment and remember, when you first gave your heart to Christ, how joyful you felt. You could hardly contain it. Do you still have it? If not, what happened? How did you lose it? Examine your life. Are you suffering from depression? Resolve to seek a doctor's care. Has the Enemy gotten to you with accusations, hurtful comments, and opinions? Is your schedule too busy to allow for time to be still? Scripture says to "resist the devil and he will flee from you" (James 4:7). One way to resist Satan is to focus on God and His character and begin to praise Him. Is there unconfessed sin in your life? Promptly confess it. God is faithful and just to forgive us our sin and cleanse us from all unrighteousness (see 1 John 1:9).

God of restoration,
I have lost my joy. Everything is colorless. Reveal to
me if it is caused by depression, and help me get
the help that is available. If it is Satan's tactic, help
me to resist him, and give me a heart to praise
You. If it is sin, show me my offense that I may
confess it before You and be restored. Thank You.
Amen.

His Forgetfulness Is Permanent

> *I will be merciful to their iniquities,*
> *and I will remember their sins no more.*
> Hebrews 8:12

G OD DEMONSTRATES HIS MERCY in His wonderful ability to forget our sins. His great love and grace are the source of His forgiveness. God's grace initiates repentance as He draws us to Himself. When we repent of our sin, He forgives us immediately. There is no sin too bad that He will not forgive except that of rejection of His Son, Jesus. He removes our sin as far as the east is from the west (see Psalms 103:12), then He cleanses us from our sins (see 1 John 1:9) and remembers our sin no more. They are removed and forgotten as if they had never happened. He gives us an opportunity to begin again with a clean slate.

Yes, there are still consequences of sin. But it is

not because He is remembering our sin and seeking ways to remind us of our mistakes. Sin has natural consequences that God allows, but when we ask for forgiveness, He forgives and forgets.

That is hard for us to understand, because we have long memories—especially when someone has wounded us deeply. We nurse our hurts, often reviewing them over and over again. They become a reference point in our life. We harbor resentment and bitterness. We may even seek subtle—or not so subtle—ways to get back at those who hurt us.

We also do the same to ourselves, beating ourselves up—unable to forgive ourselves for the sins and mistakes we have committed. We remember our failures more often than our triumphs.

God isn't that way—at all. Though our sins have wounded Him and grieve Him deeply, when He forgives He erases them permanently from His data bank, and He will not recall them. That is such a comfort to me. I am a sinner. At one time I believed I had outsinned God's grace, that He would forever shun me, leaving me to my own resources. And that He would remind me of my mistakes and sins. People did that, and I did it to myself, but God didn't. He forgave me completely, then He forgot. He gave me a clean slate so that I could start over. That's the nature of His forgiveness.

Take a moment to remember a specific sin in your life. Have you covered it over, hoping God will forget? He will not forget until you ask for His forgiveness. Right now ask Him to forgive you for that specific sin and thank Him for His forgiveness—and forgetfulness. You now have a clean slate with God— no matter how ugly your sin. And if you face consequences, ask Him to help you face them with courage.

Forgiving and forgetting God,
You are an amazing God! Thank You that You
always forgive me when I ask and give me the op-
portunity to begin again. I am glad that You forget
my sins but never forget me. I ask You to forgive
me for_____. Thank You for erasing it from Your
memory. Amen.

part ten

Realize His Restoration

He Restores Us with Love

> *God demonstrates His own love toward us,*
> *in that while we were yet sinners,*
> *Christ died for us.*
> Romans 5:8

THIS VERSE SPEAKS OF quite a remarkable concept, one I think we often don't really grasp because it is so far from our own hearts. It's one thing to try to love someone when he is difficult, messy, ugly, unlovable—that's hard enough, and most of us avoid that kind of person altogether. It's another thing to be willing to die for that person. A few, if any, would consider dying voluntarily for someone. But God did just that.

I was never a pacifist, but I place a high value on life and would never consider killing anyone. Life is a gift to be valued and respected. I never thought I could even consider taking a life—until my first child was born. Then my motherly instinct kicked in, and I knew I would take a life to protect my child, and I would give my life to protect my child. But she was my precious baby—not some difficult, messed up, ugly, unlovable being. Never would I consider having my child die for that person. But God did just that.

We are told in this verse that while you—and I—were still in sin, still ugly, still a mess, He sent His only Son to die for us. He loved us that much. He didn't require one thing of us. He formulated this plan of redemption and restoration way back in the garden of Eden when Adam and Eve first sinned. God voluntarily sent Jesus to die a brutal death to satisfy His own standard of righteousness because He wanted to restore fellowship with us. He loved us that much.

When we contemplate the depth of such radical love, such radical kindness, and such radical grace, we can celebrate the idea that God will not leave us in our sin and ugliness—there is a way back. He will restore us. That is what the cross was all about, to demonstrate His love for us—even while we were still in sin—and open the door for our complete restoration. He loves us that much. Embrace and enjoy His restoration.

Take a moment to think about the messes in your life—the mistakes, sins, regrets, lost opportunities, broken relationships. Then visualize God's love, kindness, and grace touching each ugly place, restor-

ing it to wholeness. Claim it for your life and thank
God for His wonderful love for you.

Loving Father,
I do not understand how You could love me in my
mess and sin. Thank You for doing so and giving
me the opportunity to be restored. Help me to
embrace and enjoy it every day. Amen.

He Restores Us with Compassion

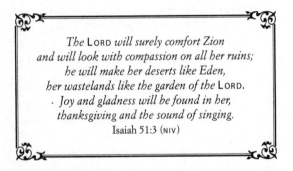

> *The LORD will surely comfort Zion*
> *and will look with compassion on all her ruins;*
> *he will make her deserts like Eden,*
> *her wastelands like the garden of the LORD.*
> *· Joy and gladness will be found in her,*
> *thanksgiving and the sound of singing.*
> Isaiah 51:3 (NIV)

WHAT A WONDERFUL PICTURE of restoration this verse paints—from ruins and wasteland to a garden with joy, gladness, thanksgiving, and singing! What made the difference? What created the change? God's compassion. God's compassion isn't the same as pity. One can feel pity and yet be passive—do nothing about it. God's compassion creates action. It is an emotion that stirs deep within Him, moving Him toward us, like the prodigal son's father, who, when he saw his son in the distance, felt compassion and sprinted toward his son, demonstrating unconditional forgiveness and full restoration. God's compassion is active.

This is one of my favorite verses. I have claimed it as my own. I know it speaks of the restoration of Jerusalem, but I have made it personal for me. When I surveyed my ruins as a result of one bad choice after another, I saw wasteland and desert. I remember reading this verse one day and being unsure if I'd ever read it before. I spent time meditating on it. I visualized my ruins—bad choices, sin, regret. Ruins are the broken bits and pieces of what used to be. Not much left. Not much useable. But then I visualized His look of compassion. His eyes see differently. He sees futures built out of wrecks. He sees hope where others see failure. God doesn't stop at ruins—it is where He begins!

Instead of ruin and wasteland, He saw a garden filled with joy, gladness, thanksgiving, and singing. I want God's eyes. Not only for myself and my life but for those I come in contact with daily. My family, friends. Even strangers. I can be so hard on others. Instead of judging and criticizing what I consider their ruins, I want to see the promise and potential God can work in them through His restoration process. God did it for me. He could have washed His hands of me, but instead He had compassion and restored me for His use and purpose. He gave me an opportunity to begin again. He will do the same for you.

Take a moment and visualize the ruined, broken places in your life—the bits and pieces of what used to be. Feel the pain and regret. Then imagine His look of compassion. The tenderness, kindness, gentleness. His look doesn't condemn or blame. He understands and loves you. He is holding out His arms, inviting you to let Him begin the restoration process. Embrace Him.

Compassionate God,
Thank You for looking at my life's wasteland with
Your love and compassion. Thank You for Your
promise of restoration. Help me to embrace that
restoration process. I want to exchange my heavy
feelings of failure and regret for joy and gladness,
thanksgiving and singing. Thank You. Amen.

He Restores Us to Our True Value

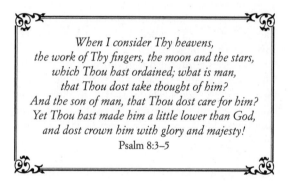

When I consider Thy heavens,
the work of Thy fingers, the moon and the stars,
which Thou hast ordained; what is man,
that Thou dost take thought of him?
And the son of man, that Thou dost care for him?
Yet Thou hast made him a little lower than God,
and dost crown him with glory and majesty!
Psalm 8:3–5

SOME YEARS AGO I was in the desert of Jordan, away from city lights at night. We were there to deliver Operation Shoebox gifts to Bedouin children. As I looked up into the vast darkness of the sky, the number of stars was beyond comprehension. Their brilliance was dazzling. I felt small and insignificant compared to the immensity of God's magnificent canopy of stars.

I can imagine King David doing much the same thing. David asked why, compared to all God had created, He would bother with humans—to think of them and care for them and give them a position close to God—a place of honor, glory, and majesty.

God gave us significance—incalculable significance. Why? He created us. He values us. He loves us. He has a purpose for us. "You are a chosen race, a royal priesthood, a holy nation, a people for God's own possession, that you may proclaim the excellencies of Him who has called you out of darkness into His marvelous light" (1 Peter 2:9).

We are significant not in our own right but in Him. We are God's creation—we have His fingerprints on our souls. He loves us. He thought we were so special that he sent His only dearly loved Son to die for us so that we might be rescued from the powerful grip of sin and its consequent devastation. He knows our sin and sees the wreckage it leaves behind. It hurts Him, but He doesn't abandon us. He restores us.

God has declared to the universe and to the angels and heavenly host that you are special to Him. You have value to God—inestimable value. You are important to Him. He freed you from the bondage of sin and called you into a life of freedom and purpose. He has restored you with glory and majesty so that you might tell others of His great love, forgiveness, grace, mercy . . . Realize your value.

Take a moment tonight and go outside to look at the stars. Feel the vastness of God's creation. Say out loud, "I am important to God. He chose me. I am significant. I have value. I am loved by the One who created all of this. He is restoring me and will use me for His purpose."

God of the universe,
I confess that inside I don't think of myself as valu-
able. Forgive me. You have given me great value
and purpose for my life. Help me to realize my
value in You. Help me to live it out daily. Thank
You. Amen.

He Restores Us Through Grace

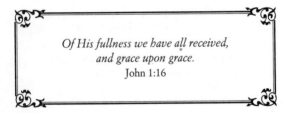

*Of His fullness we have all received,
and grace upon grace.*
John 1:16

IT'S FUN TO WATCH the TV show *Extreme Makeover: Home Edition*. The family usually has run out of means—they are desperate—and the home-improvement crew learns of their need and swoops in to restore the home in a week's time. The family did nothing to earn this. Usually a friend or neighbor has written in to tell of their need. When Ty Pennington and the crew arrive, the family is surprised and overwhelmed; it is more than they dreamed or imagined. That is grace. They did nothing to earn it, but it is given in abundance—more than they could dare to dream. What an illustration of what God does for us!

It is important to remember that God's grace is *always* working and available to us. But too often it's only when we are at the end of ourselves, when we have run out of self-effort formulas and are helpless in our wasteland of mistakes, hurts, sin, addictions, and broken relationships that we consciously realize God's grace. We don't deserve His grace. But He freely gives it. And His grace draws us to Him.

When we tell Him of our need, acknowledging Him, our hearts are opened to receive His grace, His fullness. We receive His fullness through His Holy Spirit, who dwells within us. Through that power, His power, there is restoration.

As in this earthly example, God's eternal restoration process has a plan. He sets out to accomplish this plan using people, prayer, circumstances, and our study of His Word. This is not accomplished in a week but over a lifetime as we continue to acknowledge Him and yield to His work in us. Yes, there will be some tearing down of old habits, and it can get messy, but then very creatively God sets about to restore us for His purpose and use. His work of restoration often goes beyond anything we can possibly imagine.

Restoration has its beginnings in grace. We would not even turn to God in times of devastation and brokenness if His grace did not draw us. There is nothing we can do by ourselves to be restored except to turn to Him in our need. When we hand Him our empty lives, He fills them with His fullness—grace upon grace and blessing upon blessing.

Take a moment and ask yourself where you are in need of restoration. Take a quick inventory of where you are spiritually, physically, relationally, financially, or emotionally. Are there areas of wasteland lack of discipline, apathy, isolation? Allow God's grace to draw you to Himself so that you might be given of His abundance and blessings.

God of abundant blessing,
I look at my life and see areas in real need of resto-
ration. I am worn out with self-improvement. I
fail time and again. I need Your help. Thank You
for giving me Your grace and abundant blessing.
Amen.

He Restores Us
by His Fatherhood

*Because you are sons, God has sent forth
the Spirit of His Son into our hearts, crying, "Abba!
Father!" Therefore you are no longer a slave,
but a son; and if a son, then an heir through God.*
Galatians 4:6–7

*You have not received a spirit of slavery
leading to fear again, but you have received
a spirit of adoption as sons by which we cry out,
"Abba! Father!"*
Romans 8:15

*If you then, being evil,
know how to give good gifts to your children,
how much more shall your Father who is in heaven
give what is good to those who ask Him!*
Matthew 7:11

M Y GRANDDAUGHTER IS SOMETIMES scared of the dark. She calls for her daddy to come. He doesn't hold back. He isn't angry about her need and fears. He doesn't send a stranger. He goes himself to reassure her, hold her, talk to her, soothe her fears. His comforting presence is all she wants and needs. When we are afraid of tomorrow, when anxious thoughts keep us awake, we, too, long for comfort and reassurance. We need it.

God has a tender father's heart. He paints Himself as a loving Father caring for His children. He doesn't require formality, but eagerly invites us into intimacy with Him. He says we can call Him "Daddy!" "Papa!" Those are familiar terms recognizing an intimate relationship. He invites us into that kind of familiarity and intimacy.

We are not slaves. We are not orphans. We are sons and daughters. Jesus is our brother. We are adopted into His family with full rights of being family members. God's discipline of us proves we are His children and He is our Father (see Hebrews 12:7–8). As His children, we are heirs and joint heirs with Christ (see Romans 8:16–17) to His kingdom. He gives us good things, and He gives them abundantly.

We need not be fearful of our heavenly Father. He wants us to find joy in His presence (see Psalm 16:11). It is in His loving, fatherly presence we realize restoration.

Take a moment and sit quietly. Breathe deeply and think about the kind of father you wanted and needed. Ask God to reveal Himself to you in that way, and enjoy His presence. You have nothing to fear. He loves you.

Heavenly Father,
I confess that more often than not I act like an
orphan or a slave rather than Your child. I do not
live in intimacy with You as I could. I think of You
as demanding and disappointed in me. Yet You
simply want to be in relationship with me as my
Father. You've done it all for me. Help me to relax
in Your presence and find joy and restoration
there. Thank You. Amen.

He Restores Us Through His Work

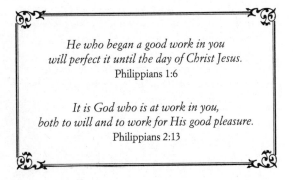

> *He who began a good work in you*
> *will perfect it until the day of Christ Jesus.*
> Philippians 1:6
>
> *It is God who is at work in you,*
> *both to will and to work for His good pleasure.*
> Philippians 2:13

IF MY CHILDREN WERE constantly trying to please me for fear I'd pull away or get angry with them, I would feel terrible. If they had a list of things they had to do to keep me happy and had to work really hard at it, I'd feel like a failure as a parent—that I had not made them feel secure in my love and acceptance. No. They are my children, and my love for them is unconditional. I want them to be motivated by love, not fear or obligation.

But all too often we tend to have a works-based relationship and not a love-based relationship with God. We know we have messed up and failed. We need restoration, but we try to get ourselves fixed up and cleaned up before we go to God. We want to make ourselves presentable.

We have the idea that we have to work really hard to please God—if we are "just good enough"—we can earn points with God. If we reform ourselves, then He will restore us. That's *not* how it works in God's kingdom.

Today's verses tell us that it is His work in us—not our work—that wills and works to please Him. Self-effort has nothing to do with it. When we give our lives to Him, He places His Holy Spirit in us to conform us to His image, and He promises that He will complete that work in us. Again, it has nothing to do with self-effort because He has done all the work for us. We just have to acknowledge, trust, and yield to His work in us. Let go of your efforts, and realize His work in you. We are free to love Him and worship Him. That's what He wants most.

Take a moment and think about God's work in your life. Can you recognize it? Can you look back over the past year and see His hand? Can you see spiritual growth? Write these times down as a record of His work in you so in the times you feel stuck or like He isn't doing anything, you can read what He did in the past. He has not quit His work in you! He will complete it. That's His promise!

Heavenly Father,
I confess that I tend to rely on self-effort. Forgive
me. I thank You that You are doing the work and
You will see it through to the end. I will be restored
just as You want me to be. Help me to acknowl-
edge, trust, and yield to Your work in me. And
please remind me often of all You've done to make
me whole. Thank You. Amen.

Day 78

He Restores Us with His Remedy

He makes me lie down in green pastures;
He leads me beside quiet waters.
He restores my soul; He guides me
in the paths of righteousness for His name's sake.
Psalm 23:2–3

WE HAVE MANY REMEDIES for all sorts of conditions. "Starve a cold and feed a fever"— or is it the other way around? Mustard plaster is said to be good for respiratory ailments. Eating a spoonful of sugar is supposed to stop hiccups. To remedy means to put right, to restore. Certainly these days many situations need remedies—from the halls of government to Wall Street, from splintered families to devastating diagnoses. But perhaps we are most desperate and in need of a remedy for our sick souls and spirits. We are spiritually weary.

God promises to restore our souls, the eternal part of us. How does He do it? What is His remedy? He makes us lie down. God knows we need rest—rest not only for the body but also for the soul. We live at such a frenetic pace that sometimes He does have to *make* us lie down because we do not do it voluntarily. We tend to think that if we do more, push harder, stay later at the office, things will get better . . . if I can just make it over the next hill . . . The more we do, the worse it gets, because it is never enough to fill the longing of our souls.

We pay a heavy price when our souls get weary and bruised, so God makes us lie down in green pastures, which indicates life. He leads us to a place of life—abundant life where our souls can be restored (see John 10:10).

God leads us beside quiet waters. He doesn't send us. He takes us Himself. He leads us to a place of soul-peace where we will find cleansing from sin, refreshing from weariness, and quenching of our thirst. He is the "living water." He invites us to drink deeply and be completely soul-satisfied.

Then He gives us purpose and direction—to go in paths of righteousness. He wants us to live lives of fulfillment and joy and peace, for His name's sake. It's not for our glory, but for His. He wants us restored and renewed so that we will be vibrant illustrations of His grace and goodness.

Take a moment and evaluate your life today. Is your soul weary? Where do you need restoration? A broken relationship? An old hurt? Spiritual dryness? Unconfessed sin?

Breathe deeply and relax. Tell God how you feel. And tell Him about each of these things. Be honest with Him and ask for His help. He is present. And He will help.

God of restoration,
I confess that the very core of me is weary, even of
what I perceive as more demands You make on
me. I long to rest in life-giving ways. I want to be
cleansed and refreshed. I want a new direction for
my life. I need You to restore my soul as only You
can. Help me. Thank You. Amen.

He Restores Us with Goodness

> *The Lord is good, a stronghold in the day of trouble,*
> *and He knows those who take refuge in Him.*
> Nahum 1:7

YEARS AGO WHEN MY father was asked to autograph a book, he would graciously sign, "God Bless You. Billy Graham. Nahum 1:7" That was his verse. As I look back over the years, I see the truth of that verse as it played out in his life. It encourages me when I get overwhelmed with ministry responsibilities, trying to balance family and work. My father found God to be good. I have too.

The prophet Nahum just simply says, "The Lord is good." The psalmist declared that "the earth is full of the goodness of the Lord" (Psalm 33:5 KJV). We see it in so many ways. His goodness is evidenced by His providence in our daily lives. Paul said, "We know that God causes all things to work together for good to those . . . who are called according to His purpose" (Romans 8:28). His grace is poured out on all mankind in creating, sustaining, providing, and protecting.

"God is good" is simple, pure, and true. It is a basic truth that we need to hear and know when we need restoration.

God is "a stronghold in the day of trouble." He guards us with His mighty power, His omniscience, His holy presence, His great faithfulness, His deep wisdom, His pure holiness, and His tender love. When we place ourselves under His protection, nothing can harm us, His children. He is sufficient for every need we bring to Him, and He is accessible for those who need restoration. He doesn't reject us when we come in times of trouble. He invites us to come.

And God knows those who take refuge in Him. When I am in trouble, I want a stronghold, a fortress, where I feel protected and safe. God is that. And when I run to Him, I don't want to be a stranger to Him—I want to be welcomed as His own. He knows me and will restore me by His goodness and love.

Take a moment and think of God's goodness to you. Remember a time when He provided for you or protected you. In what ways have you seen His goodness this week? Write them down so you don't forget.

God of goodness,
I confess that I take Your goodness for granted.
Forgive me. Thank You for being a safe stronghold
and refuge in times of trouble. Thank You for
being present to my need. Amen.

part eleven

Enjoy His Affirmation

Day 80

He Affirms Our Obedience

The word of the LORD came to me, saying,
"Before I formed you in the womb I knew you,
before you were born I set you apart;
I appointed you as a prophet to the nations."
"Ah, Sovereign LORD," I said,
"I do not know how to speak; I am only a child."
But the LORD said to me, "Do not say,
'I am only a child.' You must go to everyone
I send you to and say whatever I command you.
Do not be afraid of them, for I am with you
and will rescue you," declares the LORD.
Then the LORD reached out his hand and touched
my mouth and said to me, "Now, I have put my words
in your mouth. See, today I appoint you over nations
and kingdoms to uproot and tear down,
to destroy and overthrow, to build and to plant."

Jeremiah 1:4–10 (NIV)

INADEQUACY! IT NIPS AT our heels like a tenacious little dog that won't let go. We all experience it at one time or another.

Even Jeremiah wasn't immune. He felt that way when God told him he was going to be a prophet to the nations. Jeremiah protested. I love the fact that Jeremiah was so honest with God—no pretense, no self-reliance—just brutally honest about not feeling up to the task. He wanted God to go get someone else.

More often than not, I am asked to do things I feel inadequate to do—give a devotional to a ministry team, speak before a crowd, write a book—or sometimes it is the routine of the day that I find daunting. Planning and fixing dinner for my family when I am out of energy. Being kind to someone I don't really like.

When God calls us to do something, He equips us just as he did Jeremiah. Jeremiah's example is important to note: He was honest about how he felt, he was obedient even though he felt terribly inadequate, and he depended on God. Throughout the book of Jeremiah, we see this same pattern. We can follow his example.

So often it is in the stepping out in obedience that we experience affirmation—not before. God wants us to obey, trusting that He will supply. He meets us at the point of obedience and trust. But it is scary to step into uncertainty and inadequacy. That's okay. He will have already prepared the way and will provide what you need when you need it.

God knows us. He goes before us. He prepares the way. He makes the rough places smooth. He did that for Jeremiah. He has done that for me over and over again. And He will do it for you.

God, in His character, affirms me, blessing me and others, as I have admitted my inadequacy and shortcomings, obeyed in spite of them, and depended on Him to work in and through me. I am inadequate. But He is able.

Take a moment to think about what God has asked you to do. Tell Him how you feel about it—be brutally honest. Read His reassurance to Jeremiah, "Do not be afraid . . . I am with you." Put your name in those verses and make them your own. Determine with His help to be obedient, and invite Him to work in and through you to accomplish His purpose. Then enjoy His affirmation along the path of obedience.

All-knowing God,
Like Jeremiah, I often feel inadequate. I forget that
You know me and prepare the path ahead of me.
Forgive me for not trusting You. When I am
afraid, remind me that You are able. Today, help
me enjoy Your affirmation as You work in and
through me to accomplish Your work. Thank You.
Amen.

Day 81

He Affirms Our Participation

---

*If anyone gives even a cup of cold water
to one of these little ones because
he is my disciple, I tell you the truth,
he will certainly not lose his reward.*
Matthew 10:42 (NIV)

SOMETIMES WE THINK THE work of God is to be
done by the professionals or those more spiritual
than we are. Nothing could be further from the
truth. Just take a close look at the stories in the Bible.
God uses people we would never think of. Noah
got drunk. Abraham tried to pass his wife off as his
sister to save his own skin. David was an adulterer
and arranged for his lover's husband's death. Jacob
was a liar. Think of John the Baptist—he was sort of
an odd character! None of the twelve apostles were
men of note. They were people just like you and me.

But God has a penchant for using the imperfect, odd, broken, marginalized, and sinful. His infinite grace and mercy sees each of us, flaws and all, and chooses us to accomplish His work. He knows us and invites us to participate in His work.

For some, it might mean serving on the mission field in a faraway place. However, for most of us, His work is in the mundane and routine of our everyday lives, in our family, neighborhood, workplace, and community. It's not really complicated. It may be just giving a kind word to a coworker, a reassuring smile to the check-out clerk, being patient as we struggle to explain ourselves for the fifth time. Or it could be more involved, like walking with someone going through a divorce, an addiction, or the unexpected death of a loved one. Life is not easy. We need one another. And we need to be available to serve the simple things in the name of Jesus. It's all His work, and He prepares, empowers, and provides for us to do it.

When God trusts us to be His hands and feet helping a hurting world, there is no greater fulfillment, no greater satisfaction, than knowing we have participated with God in His work of grace, which makes a difference that counts for all eternity.

Take a moment to consider one thing you can do this week that will make a difference in the life of someone right where you live. Is it the teller at your bank who needs a smile and a great big thank-you to be reassured that she counts? Is it the single mom driving carpool who would welcome a casserole?

Maybe there's an opportunity to share God's love with a colleague. Take that step. Make a difference. Give a cup of cold water to help refresh another's soul.

God of mercy,
I come to You today, asking You to open my eyes to
the world around me. Show me what You would
have me do. Show me what that cup of cold water
is and to whom I should give it. Empower me to
make a difference doing Your work. Thank You.
Amen.

Day 82

He Affirms Our Service

*You shall receive power when the Holy Spirit
has come upon you; and you shall be My witnesses
both in Jerusalem, and in all Judea and Samaria,
and even to the remotest part of the earth.*
Acts 1:8

WHEN I WAS GOING through deep heartaches—
one right after the other—I never dreamed
that one day I would stand in front of auditoriums
full of people and share my story and all that God did
for me. I never imagined God would use my messes
to encourage others. God's grace is truly amazing. I
never want to take it for granted.

Whenever I am honored to speak at an event, I
remind myself that it isn't about me, and I ask God
to empty me of self and fill me with His Spirit so
that He can minister His grace to those in the room.

When I do it in my own strength and ability, nothing lasting comes of it. But when I step out depending on Him, He shows up in remarkable ways as His Spirit moves among the audience and touches the hearts of men and women in the room. I trust Him to do just that.

I take this ministry very seriously because I know the heartache of poor choices and sin and the pain of a broken life. Many of those who attend the Ruth Graham & Friends conferences know too. They are looking for help for themselves or someone they love. They don't need *my* help. They need the help only God's Spirit can give. I am simply His instrument, and as such, I feel affirmed and validated. I love watching Him work changing lives.

In the verse above, God says He will give His Spirit to us and that He is the source of the power we need to carry out the work He has for us to do. We do not have to do it in our own strength, but He does it through us as we make ourselves available. He will use us to tell His story of great love and mercy and to serve others in this uncertain and fearful world.

Take a moment. Breathe deeply. Tell God you are available for His service. And ask Him to fill you with His Spirit so that you might be His instrument of grace, love, and mercy to those around you. Tell Him you want Him to serve others in the unique way He has designed for you. In time, He will show you clearly just what that is and where He will do it. Acts 1:8 says He *will* do it.

Almighty God,
Thank You for loving me more than I know.
Thank You that You have allowed me to go
through many things that have designed my life
for a special purpose. Today, I ask You to fill me
with Yourself through the power of the Holy Spirit.
I make myself available for You to use me to bring
Your hope, love, mercy, and grace to others and
especially to those I come in contact with today.
I am looking forward to seeing what You will do
in and through me. Thank You. Amen.

He Affirms Our Rest

> *By the seventh day God had finished the work*
> *he had been doing; so on the seventh day he rested*
> *from all his work And God blessed the seventh day*
> *and made it holy, because on it he rested from all*
> *the work of creating that he had done.*
> Genesis 2:2–3 (NIV)

TWICE IN THIS CHAPTER it says, God "rested." Of all beings, we would think that God didn't need to rest. He is energy. Why would He rest? It wasn't because He had grown tired or weary in His labor. The great Creator, the God of the universe, was demonstrating the importance of rest.

Some of us cannot even find that word—*rest*—in our vocabulary! We work hard. Hard work is good, but we let it get the best of us. We work harder

thinking, *If I just get this one thing done, then I'll rest.*
But more often than not, that one more thing turns
into another and another and another. Minutes turn
into hours. Hours turn into days. Soon we find that
the week is gone, the month is gone, and we have not
rested. We are exhausted and find that our health, relationships, and even our work suffers. Other things
rob us of rest too—worry, indecision, anger, unre-
solved conflict, illness, and having too many irons in
the fire.

God knows we get fatigued and exhausted. God
is our example. He worked hard. Then He took time
to rest. God is our example. He rested. He made it
okay to rest!

God knows the value of rest. It restores. It re-
plenishes. It refreshes. It heals. Not to mention, we're
easier to get along with when we're rested! We need
to rest. We're designed to have periods of rest. Guess
who designed us that way? We need to feel okay
about resting. Resting is something many of us must
choose to do. We'll never find the time. We have to
make the time. It is a choice—a wise choice.

Take a moment to think about the rest you need.
What can you do in your day to ensure you get that
rest? Look at your calendar and put "rest" on it.
Maybe it means leaving work at a certain time each
day regardless of unfinished projects on your desk.
Maybe it means saying no—even at church. "No" is a
complete sentence. Without good rest, you're not
operating at your best. Give yourself permission to

turn off the phone, not answer the door, and do something you find re-creating. Choose rest. You are following God's example.

God of rest,
Thank You that You have designed me to work and
rest. Please help me to choose to take time to rest,
to see rest as a way to acknowledge You. Let me be
faithful in my work but good to my heart, soul,
and body by getting good, appropriate rest. Restore
my strength. Replenish my energy. Refresh my
spirit. Thank You. Amen.

He Affirms Our Gratitude

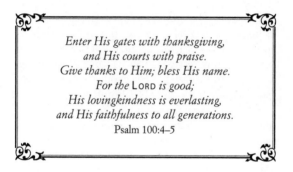

Enter His gates with thanksgiving,
and His courts with praise.
Give thanks to Him; bless His name.
*For the L*ORD *is good;*
His lovingkindness is everlasting,
and His faithfulness to all generations.
Psalm 100:4–5

THIS VERSE MENTIONS THANKSGIVING and praise. What is the difference? When we thank someone, we offer appreciation for something done for us, a kindness or favor. To praise someone is to admire and extol him. Two very different actions with the same base attitude: gratitude.

With so much uncertainty these days, there are many reasons to feel angst. Our minds turn more easily to worry and anxiety. But here God has given us an antidote for fear and anxiety: thanksgiving and praise. When we are focused on the worries of the day, it is hard to feel gratitude. When we feel like life is coming unraveled, our minds do not easily turn to thanksgiving. We don't feel like praising and worshipping. But gratitude has nothing to do with *feelings*. It is a choice, a discipline.

Do you feel like your prayers bounce off the ceiling? Do you feel as if God is distant? The key to entering into His presence is thanksgiving. That gets us inside the gate. Then praise takes us into His presence. We may not *feel* grateful, but it is good to give thanks. In this verse, He tells us some of the things for which to be grateful: His goodness, His everlasting lovingkindness, and His faithfulness.

When we are thanking Him for all that He has done for us (He loves, forgives, redeems, restores, sustains . . .) and all that He has provided (life, hope, help, strength . . .), we have no energy for worry and anxiety. Our minds are too occupied with worship and gratitude.

When we make the choice to worship instead of worry, we give the Holy Spirit room to work in our lives. When we express our gratefulness for all God had given to us, we affirm who He is, and He affirms us in our gratefulness. It frees our spirits to enter God's presence and enjoy Him.

Take a moment and make a list of things in your life for which you are grateful to Him and a list of His attributes for which you can praise Him. Read those out loud to God. Enter His presence and let

Him lift your heart and affirm who you are in Him—a child of the King, precious and wholly loved.

Loving God,
I want to enter into Your presence with praise. I
confess that far too often I am weighed down by
the cares of the day. I am worried and anxious.
Forgive me. Help me to turn my thoughts to You—
who You are and what You have done for me. I
praise You for _____ and thank You for _____.
Thank You, Lord. Amen.

Day 85

He Affirms Our Prayer

*Listen to my prayer, O God, do not ignore my plea;
hear me and answer me.*
Psalm 55:1–2 (NIV)

FROM COVER TO COVER, the Bible talks about prayer. Story after story tells us of people who faithfully prayed—Solomon, Nehemiah, Hannah, Hezekiah, Moses, Ezra, Job, Daniel, Paul, Anna, and even Jesus. They all found prayer important for living in the face of uncertainty.

Some prayers are long, thoughtful, and eloquent. Others are simple cries for help. No matter who was praying, they were all talking to God. They were talking from their hearts. They gave thanks, sang praise, confessed wrongdoing, and asked God to supply their needs, help them with problems, or heal their wounded hearts. They were very honest with God. King David prayed this, also from Psalm 55: "I am restless in my complaint and am surely distracted. . . . My heart is in anguish within me. . . . Fear and trembling come upon me; and horror has overwhelmed me" (vv. 2, 4) David talked with God truthfully and sincerely from his troubled heart. And so can we.

Prayer is a bit of a mystery. But the action of prayer is not. It is simply talking to an unseen God, to Jesus, in the way we talk to our friends, family, and colleagues. We acknowledge their presence—"Hi, Patty. It's great to see you!" We tell of our latest mishaps and celebrate our successes—"Let me tell you, the traffic was awful. In fact, this guy cut me off and almost rammed into me." We share our hopes, dreams, and concerns, often asking for help—"I'm afraid we cannot meet the mortgage payment this month." We can talk to God—pray—in the same way.

Talking to God does not require using big theological words—just basic, everyday language. My father has often told me that the prayer he prays most often is, "Lord, help me." Simple. Direct. Sometimes we don't know how or what to pray—our hearts are just too heavy. The Bible says that the Holy Spirit "intercedes for us with groanings too deep for words" (see Romans 8:26). He knows what we mean even when we don't. In response to our prayers, God answers, maybe not as we expect or when we want, but His answer is always best. Wait on Him.

When we acknowledge God in prayer, sharing

our deepest concerns, God is honored. By doing so, we give Him His rightful place in our lives. We give Him room to work. And in our heart of hearts, we experience His affirming grace of who we are as His children.

Take a moment and talk to God like you would your dearest friend. Tell God what you are thinking about. What occupies your thoughts? worries? happiness? ideas? Be honest. Tell Him where it hurts. No lofty rhetoric. Just honest truth.

O God of answered prayer,
I come to You and ask that You help me talk to You
just as I talk to a friend . . . because You are my
friend. Help me to be honest not only with You but
with myself, like King David was. I want to learn
to talk with You as a friend to a friend. Thank You.
Amen.

Day 86

He Affirms Our Redemption

> *He delivered us from the domain of darkness,*
> *and transferred us to the kingdom of*
> *His beloved Son, in whom we have redemption,*
> *the forgiveness of sins.*
> Colossians 1:13–14

Do you feel stuck? Doing the same thing over and over again? Are you in a rut and do not know how to get started in a new direction? Don't give up on yourself or your loved ones. Don't give up on God. God does not want you to be stuck. He wants you to reach your fullest potential—what He created you to be.

God is a God of action, and in this verse we see that His activity involves us. He does not want us to be stuck in the darkness of sin. He has delivered us from that—it's an already accomplished fact. A done deal. When Jesus died on the cross, He declared for all time that "It is finished." We do not have to live with fear and anxiety. We can break free from our past sin and way of life. We no longer have to be stuck. God is in the marvelous business of redemption and restoration. He will not quit on the job. He will never be too late. Sometimes, though, I think He cuts it pretty close! But we must remember that His timeline is eternal. He has a purpose for our lives—a good purpose—and He will see it through as we yield to His work in us.

Mistake after repeated mistake, I dug a deep hole. But it was never so deep that I was out of the reach of God. No one ever is—not even you. He is right there with you in the hole you have dug, longing for you to turn to Him for redemption and restoration. In my desperation, I didn't give up on Him. I continued to seek Him, to call to Him for help, to turn to Him. I also looked to others who walked with God faithfully for counsel and encouragement. In His time, God redeemed my messy life, my broken world, and restored my spirit. He gave me a "new song" so that I might share His grace with others. He gave me the privilege of using my failures to help illustrate His great redemption. That's how He works.

It wasn't easy, and it didn't happen overnight, in a few days, or even over several months. It has taken years! It was hard. I cried. I got discouraged. It seemed that I took two steps forward and three steps backward. I wish it had been easier and faster. But my story is not finished. God is still working on me—with me. I'm incredibly grateful for His redemption and His restoration, bringing me out of darkness and despair into His kingdom of help, hope, and fullness of life. That is the ultimate affirmation. I mattered to Him. And so do you!

Take a moment and ask yourself where you are stuck. Then consider God's redemption. Do you need redemption and restoration? It is available to you today through Jesus. Don't give up. Continue to seek God and trust Him in the process. He'll bring you through as you wait on Him and trust Him in the process.

God of redemption,
I confess that I am stuck and my hope is wavering.
My trust comes and goes. Help me choose to place
my faith in You to work out Your will in this situa-
tion. You are the Redeemer. You restore and re-
build broken lives. Help me believe and trust in
Your work and Your timing . . . because You are
faithful. Thank You. Amen.

part twelve

Grasp His Hope

Hope in His Help

Why are you in despair, O my soul?
And why are you disturbed within me?
Hope in God, for I shall again praise Him,
the help of my countenance, and my God.
Psalm 43:5

IN THIS PASSAGE DAVID is under stress. Earlier in the chapter we see that he must be facing some injustice. Those building a case against him are lying. He is anxious about the future. He is not just troubled; he is in despair. This is a serious situation. Things are bad and threatening to get worse. He feels as if he is in the dark.

All his efforts to find help have failed. He has reminded himself that God is his vindicator and deliverer. He asks God to shed some light on the situation. He reminds himself that God is his strength. But he feels as if God has abandoned him. When we get to that place, we do experience despair. At that point, where is hope?

Have you been there? You feel as if the situation is stacked against you. You don't know where to turn. You have tried everything you know to do, but the situation does not change and in fact seems to be getting worse. You feel that God isn't listening and has abandoned you altogether. Defeat and discouragement have led to despair.

What does David do? He stops to evaluate why he is in despair and disturbed. He reviews the situation. The scripture doesn't indicate that the situation changes, but David makes a decision. He declares, "Hope in God." David is standing on the bedrock of God's character. He is placing his hope squarely on God.

His questions are not answered. His situation has not changed. But his focus has shifted to His God. He knows God's unchanging character, and he is choosing to rely on that rather than look at the circumstances. That is David's hope.

It can be your hope today, as well. Perhaps you identify with David. You are in despair because of a failing relationship, worsening financial situation, or devastating diagnosis. Follow David's example and make the choice to hope in God. His character is unchanging. His love is enduring. His grace is sufficient. He never fails. Hope in God!

Take a moment to evaluate what is causing your despair. Review your situation, then bring God into it. Tell Him. Let Him give you His perspective. Then choose to place your hope in God. Say it out loud: "I choose to hope in God."

Giver of help,
I confess that I have let this horrible situation get the best of me. I am discouraged, defeated, and despairing of hope. I ask You to come into the situation. I choose to hope in You. Thank You that You are unchanging and worthy of my hope. Amen.

Day 88

Hope in His Confidence

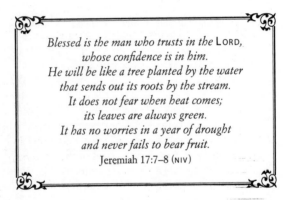

Blessed is the man who trusts in the LORD,
whose confidence is in him.
He will be like a tree planted by the water
that sends out its roots by the stream.
It does not fear when heat comes;
its leaves are always green.
It has no worries in a year of drought
and never fails to bear fruit.
Jeremiah 17:7–8 (NIV)

IT SEEMS THAT PEOPLE today are very discontent and few feel secure. Our lives are full of uncertainty and fear. Institutions and people we counted on are no longer there or have collapsed. Nothing lasts. Nothing seems to be trustworthy or stable. Life is full of change. We have lost hope. What or who can we rely on? Where can we turn?

Jeremiah in the verse above says there will be hard times. He doesn't sugarcoat it. Life is hard. But where we put our confidence and hope determines our sense of security and contentment. Too many times we want to rely on another person, a bank account, our ability, or family. Those are very fragile things in which to place confidence and hope. People fail, bank accounts evaporate, we fail, families are troubled. So where does that leave us? Where is hope? Where is hope's confidence?

Earlier in this chapter Jeremiah says that the one who places his trust in man or himself and turns away from God is wretched and will live in a parched dry place where nothing is growing or fruitful. He will not prosper, and what he does will not last. Then he contrasts the one who puts his hope in the Lord. This verse is emphatic. Confident and fortunate is the person who has placed his trust and hope in God. Not just any god—but the God of the universe, the Creator of all, the keeper and sustainer of all. The Holy One. The Eternal One. The Redeemer who loves you, forgives you, and wants to be in a personal relationship with you.

Do you want to be content? Do you want your life to count for something? Trust in God. Rely on Him. Where you place your confidence determines the hope, joy, and satisfaction you will experience in life. Relying on this great and personal God will bring eternal hope, security, and fulfillment. God is our source of hope and confidence. He never fails.

Take a moment and ask yourself where you put

your trust. This is an important question. Be honest with yourself. A relationship? money? status? government? Make the choice to put your hope and trust in God.

God of hope,
I confess that I have placed confidence in things
and people that have let me down. I have become
cynical and bitter. Forgive me. Help me to trust
You more and more each day. It isn't easy for me,
but I want to begin today. I want the hope that
trusting in and relying on You brings. I want my
life to count for things that last. Thank You. Amen.

Hope in His Promises

---

*He has granted to us His precious
and magnificent promises,
in order that by them you might
become partakers of the divine nature.*
2 Peter 1:4

To become partakers of the divine nature, we must apply His truth to our lives in all situations and claim His promises. But we cannot claim them if we do not know them. My mother used to pore over her Bible, looking for God's promises that she could claim for any given situation in her life. Whether wayward children, my father's ministry, her lack of strength for the day's tasks; nothing was too insignificant for her to find and claim a promise. For her nothing was too small for God's attention.

And she was right. God cares about the details

of our lives. When Peter writes about becoming partakers of the divine nature, he means for it to apply in every situation. We don't just partake of the divine nature at church, but at home when our children are wearing on our last nerve. Not only at Bible study, but also when we are stressed at work and want to take it out on a subordinate. When gossip starts. When we are tempted to fudge the truth. Those are the times we need to partake of the divine nature.

He makes promises to us for such times: "No temptation has overtaken you but such as is common to man; and God is faithful, who will not allow you to be tempted beyond what you are able, but with the temptation will provide the way of escape also, that you may be able to endure it" (1 Corinthians 10:13). When we feel alone and afraid: "I will never desert you, nor will I ever forsake you" (Hebrews 13:5). When we need wisdom: "If any of you lacks wisdom, let him ask of God, who gives to all men generously and without reproach" (James 1:5). When we need strength: "As thy days, so shall thy strength be" (Deuteronomy 33:25 KJV). When we need comfort: "As one whom his mother comforts, so I will comfort you" (Isaiah 66:13). When we need justice: "He will judge the world in righteousness, and the peoples in His faithfulness" (Psalm 96:13).

My mother used to say that, "All the promises of God are on the believer's side." Paul writes in 2 Corinthians 1:20, "No matter how many promises God has made, they are 'Yes' in Christ" (NIV). When we belong by faith to Christ, all the promises are ours.

Search them out. Grasp them for yourself. He is
faithful to us as we trust Him.

Take a moment and open your Bible and find a
promise that applies to your need right now. Write it
out and put your name in it. Tell God you are taking
that promise for yourself and your need.

God of promises,
My life is littered with broken promises. It is hard
for me to trust, but I ask You to help me to trust
You as I grasp hold of Your promises for my life.
Thank You. Amen.

Hope in His Love

> *I have loved you with an everlasting love;*
> *therefore I have drawn you with lovingkindness.*
> Jeremiah 31:3

SOME YEARS AGO THERE was a little book titled *Love Is a Warm Puppy.* That's a pleasant thought— puppies give so much love and pleasure. They reward you with love no matter what. They are always happy to see you. They jump and run to greet you. When you have had a bad day, they snuggle up beside you and lick your face! They love unconditionally.

Have you known a love that ended? A love that betrayed you and left you gasping for breath? Many of us have. Betrayed, rejected. With that came measureless amounts of unkindness. Cruel words, anger, abuse, and neglect. Perhaps it made you uncertain of yourself, your worthiness, your ability to make choices. Uncertain of your future. Somehow you felt as if you didn't measure up; you were lacking; it was your fault. You must be unlovable. I have felt that way. I had trusted and was betrayed at the deepest levels by the one I had given my heart to. It left deep wounds in my heart and emotions. The pain has faded, wounds healed over the years, but scars remain. Hearts mend, but scars mark the damage.

The Bible tells us that "love is from God. . . . God is love" (1 John 4:7, 8). Love is part of God's unchanging character. He is the source of love, and He has loved you with an everlasting love. That is a love that does not end. It is eternal. It is unconditional. It never forsakes. Never betrays. Never rejects. And He draws you into this everlasting love with lovingkindness.

When you are wounded and beaten up by life, you long to feel the comfort of kindness. How many times after a hard day, when you were weary and your nerves were frayed, has someone shown you a kindness that revived you and lifted your spirits? How much more so the lovingkindness of the One who knows you best! He knows just what you need and when you need it. He draws you into His embrace with tenderness and love. It's a love you can snuggle into. You are secure within His love. You can find the comfort and strength you need, and you can find rest for your weary soul. His love shelters you. But it is not a love that depends on feelings. It is a fact. God loves you.

Take a moment and think about the heartache you have experienced. Remember it. Feel it. Then ask

God to heal that pain and replace it with His unconditional, everlasting love. Sense His kindness toward
you. Reach out and grasp it for yourself.

God of everlasting love,
I confess that past hurts make it hard for me to
trust Your love. But thank You for persistently lov-
ing me with kindness anyway. Help me to know
Your secure, unconditional love in the deepest part
of me. Thank You. Amen.

Hope in His Goodness

*Every good thing bestowed
and every perfect gift is from above,
coming down from the Father of lights,
with whom there is no variation, or shifting shadow.*
James 1:17

ONE OF THE FIRST table blessings many of us learned was, "God is great. God is good. And we thank Him for our food." This verse tells us that everything good in the world, everything good in life, every perfect gift, is from Him. Goodness and perfection originate in Him.

Do we live in the light of that truth? Our world is permeated with God's gracious goodness to us, but we fail to recognize it. We fail to see the beauty of the sunset because we are in bumper-to-bumper traffic. Or we fail to marvel at the design of a rose because we are looking at the aphids. We don't take the time to be amazed at the perfection of a snow-flake because we are too busy shoveling the snow out of our way. We do not see the blessing of the rain that waters the earth because it messed up our picnic plans. We don't acknowledge God's finger-prints on our lives and world because we are so tangled up in the everydayness of life, that we don't stop and wonder at God's perfection and goodness. It is all around us.

Anxiety, worries, and uncertainties blind us to God's goodness to us. We have to make an inten-tional effort to stop and pay attention. Look for it, and as we do, we will see more of it. The eyes of our hearts will be opened, and we will be like David in Psalm 19:1: "The heavens are telling of the glory of God; and their expanse is declaring the work of His hands." The writer to the Romans said, "For since the creation of the world His invisible attributes, His eternal power and divine nature, have been clearly seen" (Romans 1:20). It's there to be seen. By ac-knowledging it, you grasp it for yourself.

Take a moment and write down the things around you that reveal God's goodness to you today. Look for a perfect gift He has given you. Thank Him and ask that He open your eyes to see even more. Make time each day to write down at least one good thing God did for you that day—a "blessing book."

Good and perfect God,
Forgive me for being so busy and worried about
my life that I fail to see Your goodness and perfect
gifts to me on a daily basis. Open my eyes that I
might see You in and around the everydayness of
my life. I want to acknowledge and praise You for
Your abundant goodness to me. I grasp it now as
my own. Thank You. Amen.

Hope in His Joy

> *May the God of hope fill you*
> *with all joy and peace in believing,*
> *that you may abound in hope by the power*
> *of the Holy Spirit.*
> Romans 15:13

ONE WORD I WILL always associate with my mother is *joy*. Mother exuded joy. Not because her life was easy—far from it. With five children to rear, a home to run, bills to pay, not enough money to meet the demands, being expected to act and dress appropriately although she was never trained for her position, a husband who was married to his ministry and often preoccupied, she chose joy rather than self-pity. She chose to grasp His joy. We choose joy when we commit our lives to Christ, trusting the God of hope to work in us and through our circumstances for His purpose. That's what my mother did.

This verse says, "Fill you with all joy"—that's what we want. To be filled with all joy. How do we get it? It comes from God who is the fountain of joy. In this verse hope is linked to joy and peace and believing. If we have hope, then we will have joy—not necessarily happiness—and peace—not the absence of conflict but the assurance that we have the resources to meet our need. We become hopeless when we think the situation is overwhelming and we do not have what it takes to meet it. Hope seems lost. Joy can be dampened, if not swallowed up, by selfishness, regret, shame, and anxiety. These things crowd out joy.

What role does believing play? Peace and joy can be fragile when based upon circumstances. When we believe in the God of hope, our peace and joy are firmly planted on the bedrock of God's unchanging character and come to us through the Holy Spirit, who dwells in us. Believing is faith. Peace and joy are unassailable when based in faith. "Faith comes from hearing, and hearing by the word of Christ" (Romans 10:17). We need to study and know what Scripture says so that faith grows and our joy and peace are rooted in the eternal. When we make the choice to trust in the face of overwhelming circumstances, the Holy Spirit gives us joy and peace. By believing, we grasp His joy.

Take a moment—do you have joy and peace and

hope? If not, why? What is crowding them out? Tell God and choose to grasp His joy by believing His Word and relying on the Holy Spirit to guide you.

God of hope,
Forgive me when I falter in my trust of You. I want to be filled with joy and peace. I want to believe Your Word and abound in hope. Help me to grow in my faith. Thank You. Amen.

Hope in His New Beginnings

Behold, I will do something new,
now it will spring forth; will you not be aware of it?
I will even make a roadway in the wilderness,
rivers in the desert.
Isaiah 43:19

CHURCHES HAVE REVIVALS. STORES have "grand openings." Products are labeled "new and improved." We like new clothes, a new car, a new house. We like to try what is new. Every New Year's people make resolutions. They hope that with a new year they can get a fresh start and break old habits or start new ones. We celebrate new beginnings: a marriage, a new home, a new baby, graduations— passages and milestones that mark our lives.

God, too, marks new beginnings. He made a new covenant with us, "This cup which is poured out for you is the new covenant in My blood" (Luke 22:20). We celebrate this every time we take communion. When we are in Christ, He says we are "a new creature; the old things passed away; behold, new things have come" (2 Corinthians 5:17).

He is going to establish a new heaven and a new earth (see Revelation 21:1). He will give us a new name (see Revelation 3:12). God is about newness.

God's plans are about newness. The world had God pegged as to what they expected He would do. But He surprised everyone. When He broke into history, He came as a brand-new baby. No one expected that. They were expecting a conquering hero; instead, they got a suffering servant. They had not heard what the prophets had foretold, so they missed His coming. They misunderstood His purpose and message, and so they crucified Him. They did not expect His resurrection the third day or the power of the Holy Spirit at Pentecost. God is full of surprises. He loves to do new things.

And He wants to do a new thing in you. Even the impossible—like making rivers in the desert. And difficult—roadways in the wilderness. Are you in a desert place right now? Everything seems dried up and old. You see no refreshing. Are you in a wilderness and see no way out? Everywhere you look is just sandy wasteland. God says He is going to do something new. It will spring forth—surprise you— and you will then see it.

I know He will do it for you. He did it for me. I was in a desert place, a wilderness of mistakes, sin, and brokenness. I was sure God would never be able to use me. I felt I had outsinned His grace. Little did I know He would "put a new song in my mouth, a song of praise to our God; many will see and fear, and will trust in the LORD" (Psalm 40:3). God is a God of new beginnings—ask Him for yours. Grasp it.

Take a moment and breathe deeply. Imagine all the old, dried-up stuff in your life—the regret, the shame, the sin and mistakes—the things that have you bound to the old. Now imagine Jesus breaking those chains and sending you out with a new purpose and vision for your life, giving you a new beginning. Reach out and grasp it!

God of new beginnings,
I confess that I am stuck in old habits, old ways. I
don't have a sense of purpose or vision. I need a
fresh start. I need refreshing and revival that
comes from You. Please help me to realize Your
way in my life. Thank You. Amen.

part thirteen

Anticipate His Plans

His Plans
for Your Transformation

> *We all, with unveiled face beholding as in a mirror*
> *the glory of the Lord, are being transformed into*
> *the same image from glory to glory,*
> *just as from the Lord, the Spirit.*
> 2 Corinthians 3:18

To SEE THE GLORY of the Lord, we have to take our masks off. The mask of pretense—that we have it all together, we don't need anyone, we aren't in pain, we aren't afraid. We all have masks of one type or another to protect us from people knowing us too well so they can't hurt us. Some call it a "game face"; others call it a "public persona." Early on, parents tell their children to mind their "p's and q's." These masks keep people from getting too close and we think they protect us but ultimately they leave us feeling more alone and afraid.

Sometimes our masks have been in place for so long that we forget they are there. They keep people from getting too close, but they also keep us from getting too close to God. When we are wearing masks, we aren't being honest with ourselves or God. We are trying to hide who and what we really are. We are also more inclined to sin when we are wearing masks, because we are not being who God created us to be.

God knows who we really are, and He loves us. He wants to reveal Himself in us—like a mirror reflection—but He cannot do that with the mask in the way.

Adam and Eve didn't have to wear masks. We are told in Genesis that they were naked—physically, emotionally, spiritually—and not ashamed. They had been created in His image and reflected His glory. They walked and fellowshipped with God in the garden. Then they chose to sin, and suddenly they knew they were naked and tried to hide from God because they were ashamed. Masks are a result of sin and our efforts to cover up.

That is not what God wants for us. His purpose, His desire, is to reveal His glory in us. As we take the masks off, being honest with Him and with ourselves, we can anticipate being transformed by the power of His Spirit to reflect who He is in us.

Take a moment and make a list of the different images you try to create for the public. How successful are you? What are the consequences? Be honest with yourself and God. Ask God to help you remove your mask so He can be seen more clearly in and through you.

God of transformation,
I confess that I am afraid of people knowing what
I am really like. I hide my true self behind layers of
pretense. This does not honor You. Forgive me. I
want to be transformed by your Spirit to reflect
more of You. Thank You. Amen.

His Plans for Being Present

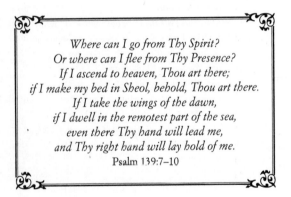

Where can I go from Thy Spirit?
Or where can I flee from Thy Presence?
If I ascend to heaven, Thou art there;
if I make my bed in Sheol, behold, Thou art there.
If I take the wings of the dawn,
if I dwell in the remotest part of the sea,
even there Thy hand will lead me,
and Thy right hand will lay hold of me.
Psalm 139:7–10

SMALL CHILDREN GO THROUGH a stage where they experience separation anxiety. They fear that their parent will leave and not come back. There is a wonderful children's book, *The Runaway Bunny*, which tells the story of a bunny who decides to leave in a variety of ways—fly into the sky, swim out to sea—each one to test his limits and his mother's love. But his mother assumes a variety of forms: a cloud, a sailboat . . . so that she will be near her child. She assures him that she will go to the ends of the earth to track him down. She gives him security to try his wings, test the limits, explore what's out there. Children identify with the story, and it brings comfort and reassurance that no matter what they do, wherever they go, their parent will be there.

We all have the same fear and need. We fear that our sin can take us beyond the presence of God—beyond God's love and care for us, and we need reassurance that God will not abandon us. We want to hear, *I love you. I will track you down. I'll do what I need to do to find you and bring you home.* The Bible is the story of God's relentless pursuit of us. The parable of the lost sheep illustrates this so well. The shepherd leaves the ninety-nine in the fold to go search and rescue the one lost sheep. From the time Adam and Eve first sinned in the garden of Eden, God set in motion a plan to redeem us back to Himself that culminated in the death and resurrection of Jesus, His only Son.

We are never alone, rejected, or abandoned. Never. We may feel like it at times, but the fact is that we are not. We may try to run away from God, get as far away as possible, but His presence is inescapable. The above scripture speaks so directly to the fact that we cannot get away from God's presence. We can anticipate and count on His presence. He is always with us—even when we want to flee from Him, He is there. He will pursue us because He loves us and longs to be in relationship with us.

Take a moment and think about the ways your sins have taken you away from God. Confess and repent of those sins. Slowly reread the above scripture and let it sink in. God is present with you. You can anticipate His presence at all times.

Pursuing Father,
Thank You for your inescapable presence. Thank You for Your constant pursuit and love of me regardless of my disobedient and sinful ways. I am sorry for my selfish choices and sin. I ask Your forgiveness. Thank You for Your open arms and Your forgiving grace. Amen.

His Plans for Your Restoration

> *I will restore to you the years the locust hath eaten.*
> Joel 2:25 (KJV)

SOMETIMES WE FIND OUR lives in ruins. We are broken and feel ruined. No doubt the apostle Peter felt that way after he denied Jesus (see Matthew 26:69–75).

Look who he had been. He was a close intimate of Jesus—he, James, and John were in Jesus' inner circle. Jesus was his best friend. Peter was present at the transfiguration. He heard Jesus preach the Sermon on the Mount and participated in the feeding of the five thousand. His mother-in-law was miraculously healed by Jesus' tender touch. He witnessed many miracles performed by Jesus and sat at Jesus' feet as He taught about the kingdom of God. He fished with the Lord. He partied with Him. He saw

Lazarus raised from the dead. He saw demons cast out of people. He knew Jesus' power. He was the first to declare that Jesus was the Son of God, and Jesus told him that He would build His church on Peter. Peter said he would die for Jesus. He had been there when Judas betrayed Him—he had cut the ear off of the high priest's servant in defense of Jesus. Peter followed Jesus at a distance when He was arrested and taken to the high priest's house.

He had a bright future ahead. Until . . . following Jesus required him to perhaps risk his life. As he sat in the courtyard with the soldiers while Jesus was being questioned, he denied the Lord three times—cursing that he didn't know Him. At that point Jesus turned to look at Peter.

Talk about feeling ruined! The scripture says he went out and wept bitterly. The remorse, the guilt, the shame of it all fell on him. How would he ever face himself much less the others? Where could he go?

But God is a restorer. He loves to restore lives—that is His specialty. We are told that three days later, after the resurrection, Jesus asks for Peter by name to meet him in Galilee. It is there that Jesus gives him the chance to reaffirm his love for Him three times. Not only is Peter given a chance to affirm his love, but Jesus gives him a responsibility. Jesus sees Peter as qualified in his brokenness to minister to others. And shortly thereafter a broken but restored Peter is the keynote speaker at Pentecost!

Many of us have experienced brokenness in some form—through our own choices, the choices of others, or by life. God doesn't leave us there. If we bring the broken pieces to Him, He makes from them something He can use in the lives of others. He did it for me; He will do it for you. He doesn't stop at ruins; it is where He begins. He restores beautifully. He gives us the opportunity to begin again.

Take a moment and ask yourself where you need restoration in your life. Ask the Holy Spirit to gently reveal things to you that need His restoration, and release them to Him. Give Him permission to work in you and the situation, in His time, to restore in a way that brings Him glory.

God of restoration,
Thank You for telling Peter's story. It gives me
hope. Thank You for not leaving me in my ruins.
You want to give me a chance to begin again. I
want to cooperate with You, but I need Your help.
Amen.

His Plans for Granting You Grace

*Let us therefore draw near with confidence
to the throne of grace,
that we may receive mercy and find grace
to help in time of need.*
Hebrews 4:16

IMAGINE WITH ME IF you will: You have been
caught speeding in a school zone for the second
time. You know the consequences. This time it will
affect your ability to drive because the judge told you
last time not to come again to his court. But there
you are. The courtroom is intimidating with its tall
ceilings, high judge's bench, hard wooden chairs.
It is austere. There is no place to hide. Every sound
echoes. People whisper. You look for a friendly face
but see the familiar faces of the arresting officer and

the judge you stood in front of before. They look unsympathetic.

You are afraid—beyond afraid. Your life will be altered by the decisions made here. You replay in your mind your offense. You play the "if only" game: "If only I had left the house earlier . . . If only I had slowed down at the school zone . . . If only the policeman had been taking a coffee break . . ." But it is too late. The hour has come to face the judge and his sentence. You long for mercy but expect severe justice. This is how an earthly court operates.

Imagine with me, if you will, the heavenly courtroom. All the sins you have committed suddenly come to mind, and you know you are guilty. You approach the Judge and wait to hear His sentence of conviction. He looks at you with eyes of mercy and declares that He finds no sins on your account. His Son has paid the price, and you are free to go. As you turn to leave, you notice the bright colors emanating from the throne like a rainbow, a glassy sea, gold crowns, white robes, and living creatures crying out, "Holy, Holy, Holy is the Lord God, the Almighty." The elders are worshipping God. It is awesome. All the faces in the crowd are friendly and welcoming, none more so than that of His Son, who paid the price for your freedom.

You went to the throne of grace and did, indeed, find mercy and grace for your need just as He promised.

Take a moment to reflect on the two courtroom

scenes. In both situations you are clearly guilty. In the earthly courtroom you find judgment, but in the heavenly courtroom you always find grace and mercy. Take a piece of paper and write down your sins that come to mind. Read the verse again and write across the paper, "Mercy given." Take time to praise and thank God.

Merciful Judge,
I confess I am guilty and have sinned against You.
Thank You for Your grace and mercy in sending
Jesus, Your Son, to pay my debts so that I might
live free of condemnation and shame. Amen.

His Plans for Returning

> *Looking for the blessed hope*
> *and the appearing of the glory of*
> *our great God and Savior, Christ Jesus . . .*
> Titus 2:13

WE EXPERIENCE ANXIETY, FEAR, heartache, shame, regret, stress, and pain in this life. Life is hard. We may often feel as David did when he cried, "Oh, that I had wings like a dove! I would fly away and be at rest" (Psalm 55:6). Many times as we look at the state the world is in—wars, financial crises, epidemics, natural disasters, lack of core values, dishonest leaders, great uncertainty—the future is depressing. We fear tomorrow for ourselves, our children, and grandchildren.

But that is not the end of the story! As my mother often said, "I've read the last chapter, and I know who wins!" When we read this scripture, we know our future. Jesus is coming back to gather His people to Himself! What an exciting day that will be. Each year brings us closer to that day.

Since Jesus' day, people have been wondering when He will return. I am not one to give a timetable or say one thing will happen before something else happens. I think it is easy to get sidetracked with those kinds of speculations. Even Jesus said that no one knows but the Father, "But of that day or hour no one knows, not even the angels in heaven, nor the Son, but the Father alone" (Mark 13:32). Our task is to anticipate His return. We are to live our lives in light of His return. How do we do that? We live our lives in dependency on Him and obedience to His Word.

I anticipate that day when "the Lord Himself will descend from heaven with a shout, with the voice of the archangel, and with the trumpet of God" (1 Thessalonians 4:16). I have no idea what that shout will be, but I like to think He will call my name: "Ruth, I have come. Ruth, I am here. Ruth, I have come to take you to be with Me in heaven." And accompanying Him will be those who went before me—my mother and friends and family—eagerly awaiting my arrival. What a great day of reunion!

Take a moment and thank the Lord for His promise to return. Think of ways you might actively anticipate that day, and write them down. Post that list in a place where you will see it as a reminder of His return and living in light of that day.

God of all times,
Thank You for the promise that You are going to
return to gather Your people to Yourself. Forgive
me for often forgetting that. Help me to live my life
in obedience, faithfully depending on You. Thank
You. Amen.

Day 99

His Plans for Your Gifts

Go therefore and make disciples of all the nations,
baptizing them in the name of the Father
and the Son and the Holy Spirit.
Matthew 28:19

THIS COMMAND ISN'T JUST for religious professionals or the very spiritual; it is for you and me. God has given us purpose while we are on earth awaiting His return. He told us to go make disciples of all nations. "Disciples" means followers of Christ. "All nations" means everyone. We are to anticipate building His kingdom everywhere we go.

What does that mean? It means to be ready to use your gifts wherever and anywhere you are able for God's kingdom. It means to anticipate opportunities. Do we preach everywhere? Do we carry our

Bibles everywhere? Do we accost people on the street or the person sitting beside us on the airplane or standing behind us in the grocery line? Not necessarily. Sometimes that is offensive. But I do have friends who can strike up a conversation with just about anyone and turn it into an opportunity to share the gospel. What a gift!

God has designed each of us for service to Him—He has given us each gifts for that purpose. Paul mentions the gifts of teaching, preaching, making miracles, healing, and others. Paul's list is not a complete list. There are gifts like a listening ear, keeping a confidence, encouragement, and a willingness to intercede for others in prayer. People assume I can preach because my last name is Graham and my father is a well-known preacher. God did not give me that gift. But I can cook! I can entertain and welcome people into my home to get to know them and provide a safe place for them to be themselves. I can use that gift to make disciples.

I cannot go to all nations, but I can go into my neighborhood and start there. These days neighborhoods are so ethnically diverse that you can reach many nations just by being neighborly. When I hear an ambulance or fire siren, I pray for the people involved. When I hear of a need, I can pray and take soup. My husband likes to say, "God uses ordinary people in extraordinary ways."

I believe you build His kingdom by finding out what gift or gifts God has given you and using them to reach out to others. Yes, God has given us work to do for Him that has eternal results. Anticipate opportunities.

Take a moment and think about the gifts God has given you and how you might use one of them to reach out to someone around you. Write that person's name down, and make a plan to start with a small step this week. Maybe just a phone call or encouraging note.

Giver of gifts,
I confess that I am not sure what gifts I have that
You can use for building Your kingdom. Please
help me discover them and then anticipate ways I
might use them to reach others for You. Amen.

His Plans for Your Abundant Life

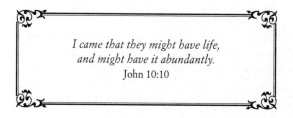

> *I came that they might have life,*
> *and might have it abundantly.*
> John 10:10

S O OFTEN WE THINK that if we leave the choice to God or turn our lives over to Him, He will choose the hardest and most difficult lives imaginable for us. We imagine Him as harsh and a hard taskmaster. That is a lie straight from Satan himself. I believe the abundant life is not a way around the hard things of life, the uncertainties, the heartache. I believe that the abundant life is the way through them. Nothing exempts us from difficulties and hardships. We live in a fallen world. And while we may try to insulate and protect ourselves from harsh realities, we can't—they come to all of us at some point in life.

It is the hard things, the difficulties, the heartaches, and the pain that develop us into people of depth and character. We grow strong in the struggle. We have to dig our roots deep into the rich soil of God's character. We learn to live in the face of our pain, leaning on Him to be our all in all and we grow stronger for it. We get to know Jesus intimately. That in itself is a great reward.

"Things which eye has not seen and ear has not heard, and which have not entered the heart of man, all that God has prepared for those who love Him" (1 Corinthians 2:9). A variation of this verse appears two other times in the Bible (in Isaiah 64 and 65) so God must want us to know and understand it. It is a promise that often is associated with heaven, but I believe it is for the here and now. We can experience it in everyday life now—this side of heaven.

We have God's promise that we have not seen or heard or even imagined all that God has planned for those who love Him. But we have to change our mind-set from the temporal to the eternal. He isn't promising that we will win the lottery or have good health or a trouble-free life. He is promising things far more lasting and important, things like fulfillment in a life of service, joy in the face of grief, wealth of relationship with Him, peace in uncertainty. No, He doesn't promise an easy pain-free life, but the rewards of loving Him and following after His ways are unimaginable! Anticipate the abundant life.

Take a moment and make a list of the ways God has enriched your life—especially during the hard times. Thank Him for them. Praise Him for being the God who gives us far more than we could have imagined.

Heavenly Father,
So often I seek ways around the hard things in life.
I fail to see the potential for my growth in You and
am content with things as they are. But You have
much more for me—so much more. Help me to
live in the anticipation of the abundant life.
Thank You. Amen.